BLACK LONDONERS 1880–1990

The seamstress Esther Bruce (left) with her stepmother and father, *see* p. 16.

BLACK
LONDONERS
1880–1990

S U S A N   O K O K O N

SUTTON PUBLISHING

Sutton Publishing Limited
Phoenix Mill · Thrupp · Stroud
Gloucestershire · GL5 2BU

First published 1998

Cover: clockwise from top left: Esther Bruce with her stepmother and father, *see* p. 17; Black tailor, *see* p. 53; John, son of President of Liberia, *see* p. 85; Paul Keynes Douglas, *see* p. 90; the mother of Cherry Groce, *see* p. 117. *Half-title photograph*: Rudolph Dunbar, *see* p. 24. *Title photograph*: Anti-apartheid march, 1982, *see* p. 123.

British Library Cataloguing in Publication Data
A catalogue record for this book is available from the British Library.

SBN 0-7509-1548-X

Typeset in 10/12 Perpetua.
Typesetting and origination by Sutton Publishing Limited.
Printed in Great Britain by Ebenezer Baylis, Worcester.

This book is dedicated to my mother Mrs K.A.M. Okokon (SRN, SCM), whose ability to memorize the family tree of a nation has always been a source of inspiration and wonderment to me. Her narrative style has breathed life into the whole notion of history.

The author and the publishers would like to thank the editors and staff of the following publications without whose cooperation this book would not have been possible.

Caribbean Times incorporating African Times

CONTENTS

South African gold mine, 1933. South African gold mines featured in the First Pan-African Conference, 23–25 July 1900 in Westminster town hall. The event was aimed at '[taking] steps to influence public opinion on existing proceedings and conditions affecting the Natives in the various parts of the Empire, viz., SOUTH AFRICA, WEST AFRICA and the British WEST INDIES'.

Native crockery sellers, 1907. Historically Black craftsmen and women and traders have occupied an important role in the self-determination and economic independence of the Black peasantry. Many Black women retained, or were handed down, craft skills from their African heritage and evolved and adapted those to the demands of the 'new world'.

INTRODUCTION

This book comprises a collection of brief biographies of Black Londoners, 1880–1990. The aim is not to argue a case, but to remind readers of the contributions of Black Londoners to the twentieth century, as we embark upon the twenty-first. This book does not pretend to be comprehensive.

In the nineteenth century, Black Londoners consisted of the sons and daughters of earlier generations of Black people, students, workers from the 'old Empire' or the British colonies in the West Indies, and the soon to be 'new Empires', in Africa, whose annexation was already being planned among the 'European powers'. One group that is often forgotten in our focus on Africa's disempowerment, at this time, is the African kings and queens, and their emissaries. Church Missions were another motivating force for Black people who came to London, many of whom were to play an active part in the evangelical movement, such as Sylvester Williams and George Mappike, taking with them the hopes of a community, and acting as their agents in the wider world.

In addition many Black children were raised in military or naval schools which acted as schools cum orphanages, and technical colleges. Black Londoners also featured among the very poorest in society. In the late nineteenth century, we begin to see attempts of social reformers such as Booth to define the poor. At this time anthropologists also attempted to classify 'types' among the poor. It is often the case that poor people are described as being a 'race' apart. While some may interpret this to indicate the social scorn heaped among the poverty stricken, it may also be supposed that at least some of the poor may have African physiological traits.

There is nothing inevitable about history. History consists of those bits of the past that someone had the knowledge, interest, foresight and ability to record for future generations. The telling of the Black history of London, ancient and modern, is more flawed than most historical narratives for several reasons, some personal and individual, others institutional and cultural. The story of Dr George Rice and schoolmistress Mary Lucinda Rice illustrates the problems of continuity in historical record-keeping, even in the case of exceptional individuals. A Black man was clearing a house for the local authority, the contents of which were to be consigned to the local rubbish dump. He came across a discovery as shattering to him as the discovery of a pharaoh's tomb was to the early Egyptologists. He came to the conclusion that what had been classified as 'junk' by the local authority was in fact Black gold. It was a series of papers and artefacts documenting the life of a Black doctor and his family who lived in Woolwich in the 1890s – the Rice family. We know of Dr Rice because his daughter, Miss Mary Lucinda Rice, had recognized the importance of keeping a family archive. The trouble was, she had neither family nor anyone else left to value her own or her family's possessions when she died. But for fate, or the wise stranger sent to clear her house, we would not know anything about Dr Rice or Mary Lucinda Rice.

The story of the Rice family challenges what we might have expected of the life of a Black man and woman in Edwardian Britain. Dr Rice ran a series of hospitals in the north of England and in south London, and was a highly respected man within the upper echelons of the medical profession. His daughter, Lucinda Rice, ran a preparatory school. Their descendants are White people who are extremely proud of their ancestors, especially since they began to find out more through researching their family history some years ago.

Throughout Britain there have probably been thousands of people like Dr Rice. Perhaps not all of them were as accomplished as he was, but their stories are none the less important in telling us about the Black history of the British Isles. Every year hundreds of White British are discovering African ancestry from the waves of immigration centuries ago. Black people must also lay claim to this past. A multicultural community must, by definition, make all its members proud and confident about the achievements of its Black citizens, both nationally and internationally, wherever they are found.

THE NATURE OF 'GREATNESS'

To be recorded by official institutions, an individual or an event must at some stage be deemed to be of particular value to society. The notion of 'greatness' is a highly subjective one, governed by considerations of race, class and gender, and by a person's or event's place within our affections. Despite the enormous fame of Mrs Seacole in the nineteenth century, the deaths of her friends and supporters and her lack of dependants, caused her place in British history to be diminished. Her age was preceded by a period of imperial expansion and control when ideology sought to justify this expansion by diminishing the achievements of racial groups considered 'inferior'.

In this context, the contribution of Africans and their African-British descendants was not valued. It was therefore not surprising that with the growth and expansion of museums in the nineteenth century, the reputation of those such as Mrs Seacole, who was a Jamaican woman of mixed race, gave way to the new heroes and heroines of 'pure European blood', of the British Empire. The status of Mary Seacole as a British heroine has been enhanced by the growth in Britain of a multicultural society which has encouraged Black people to seek the roots of their past, in Britain as well as in Africa and the West Indies.

ONE FAMILY'S STORY

In the modern age, the inclusion within this book of the Moodys, an influential Black family which has spanned the twentieth century, gives us new insights into a dynamic range of community and personal survival strategies available before the advent of the mass immigration in the 1950s, and the more recent gestures and safeguards afforded by race relations laws and policies.

Members of the Moody family have been included in several chapters in this book, demonstrating an almost breathtaking and wholly inspiring self-confidence and self-assertion, which, with hindsight, have proved to be among the most powerful weapons in the face of ignorance and prejudice. Theirs is a story which raises issues of the interplay of the politics of class, gender and race.

Cynthia Moody was an early exponent of international television and cinema advertising. Yet this heroine of the modern age is the first to acknowledge the debt owed to her forebears, such as Harold Moody, an uncle, who by confronting injustices on behalf of his family and community as a founder of the League of Coloured Peoples made survival for many Black Londoners tolerable.

THE PATH OF 'PROGRESS'

Researching the biographical narratives of this book, it became clear that progress for Black Londoners is not a linear process in which rights increase with time. An alternative reading would suggest the possibility of progress, privileges and enlightenment coexisting alongside extreme prejudice. Samuel Coleridge-Taylor, composer and musician, recalls a racial assault by a fellow student at the Royal College of Music, London. The same day, Coleridge-Taylor was described by the Principal as among the most gifted students in the College. Assaults on his person were not rare occurrences. One day Coleridge-Taylor would be conducting an élite orchestra, performing his own composition, the next he would be spat at in the streets. His answer was the pursuit of excellence, and to use his privileged position to campaign for the rights of his fellow Black citizens of London and the British Empire.

In the 1940s, Rudolph Dunbar was to take up Coleridge-Taylor's baton as the next Black man to conduct at the Royal Albert Hall. However, despite Dunbar's historic contribution to classical music before and immediately after the Second World War, he was shunned by the musical establishment from the 1950s until his death. Ian Hall, his nephew, himself a conductor and composer, recalls an incident at one post-performance reception at the Royal Albert Hall when Dunbar, then an old man, congratulated a young clarinettist upon his performance. When asked what inspired him to take up the clarinet as a career, the young man replied, 'A book on the clarinet written by a man called Dunbar.' Dunbar said nothing, smiled and moved on. The irony was not lost on Hall, who later commented, 'Dunbar's pupil was able to perform, when the master was destined to be shut out from the world of classical music.' Dunbar was to spend the rest of his life as a journalist and political activist, fighting the system which deprived him of his first love – classical music.

It is an intention of this book to acknowledge the presence of Black Londoners in spaces from which many may have assumed them to have been excluded. Many of these careers do not contradict the fact of racial exclusion but add new understanding to sets of circumstances in which enormous achievement, creativity and enterprise are able to flourish, often like oases in deserts of despair.

Carting molasses, 1909. Sugar was transformed from a luxury to a household necessity by the West Indian economy which was based on the commodity and fuelled by the labour of Africans, specifically transported as slaves to meet this 'industrial need'. In 1775 rum, a by-product of sugar manufacturing, replaced brandy as the spirit ration of the British Navy. Barbados, the Leeward Islands, Jamaica and the Bahamas were the first British colonies in the Caribbean in the seventeenth century. The Windward Islands, Trinidad and Guyana were acquired in the eighteenth century. Well before the Industrial Revolution sugar plantations were run along proto-industrial lines with royal encouragement and regulation of West Indian Black slavery from London.

CHAPTER ONE

THE ARTS, ENTERTAINMENT & SPORT

A close reading of the biographies of Black Londoners often reveals the complex nature of fame and achievement – nowhere more so than in the realm of the arts and entertainment.

Ronald Moody, for example, became one of Britain's most outstanding postwar sculptors, yet dentistry had originally brought him from Jamaica to England in 1923 to study at King's College, London. Moody was intending to develop a dental practice alongside his brother's medical practice in Peckham. Inspired by Egyptian artefacts at the British Museum, however, Moody felt compelled to sculpt. His life defies narrow categorization; he was a regular exhibitor at the Royal Academy and the Royal Society of Portrait Sculptors, and sat on its Governing Council from 1950. Yet he was also a member of the Caribbean Artists Movement, based in London from 1967.

Uzo Egonu was an artist, printmaker and art history scholar, who came to Britain at the age of thirteen and later became one of the most internationally recognized Black artists in Europe. A Londoner who lived and worked in Hampstead and Wembley, Egonu received some of the world's major art prizes. He died in 1996, and how many people beyond artistic circles are truly aware of his legacy? Uzo Egonu's story suggests some of the reasons why Black Londoners' historical contributions have often gone unrecognized. He was born in Nigeria and, like so many Black Londoners, his place of origin has made it more difficult for his contribution to his new home to recognized. Also, Uzo Egonu occupies a contested cultural space. He simply does not fit easily into Western notions of the African artist as being 'primitive', untutored and non-intellectual. That he studied both African and Western art history traditions, sought to concentrate upon universal themes, and was received internationally, has rendered Uzo Egonu almost invisible as a Black Londoner.

The career of Elisabeth Welch suggests another kind of invisibility which successful

Black Londoners engaged in the arts, entertainment and sport may still face. Historical narratives tend to focus on ancient or relatively recent historical figures. Those who predate our living memory but have not yet been included in historical texts are victims of a kind of cultural amnesia. Elisabeth Welch has been a prominent member of London's theatrical community since the 1930s. She was one of the first Black people to have her own BBC radio series, *Soft Lights and Sweet Music*, which made her a household name in Britain. The illusion of showbiz glamour has been almost too successful in concentrating on her celebrity status at the expense of her status as a Black woman in a highly competitive and commercial enterprise in 1930s Britain.

In Elisabeth Welch's case, as in so many in this chapter on the arts, entertainment and sport, our attention is drawn to the end product or the surface personality, and not to the often very complex social and historical circumstances which led to their emergence. With greater curiosity, and more research, we may come to realize that most of these personalities carry within their stories access to yet more hidden histories of London.

Orlando Martins in *Where No Vultures Fly* (1951). Born in Nigeria in 1899, he settled in London in 1919, earning a living as a porter at Billingsgate fish market, a snake charmer with Lord John Sanger's Circus (Olympia), a night watchman, a kitchen porter, a sailor in the Merchant Navy and a ballet extra at the Lyceum. Martins eventually became the foremost Nigerian actor in Britain, performing on stage, screen, television and radio. He came to prominence through such films as *West of Zanzibar* (1929) and Paul Robeson's *Sanders of the River* (1936), and as Toussaint L'Ouverture at the Westminster Theatre. When British film competed with Hollywood, Orlando featured in *The Four Feathers* (1939) and the technicolour fantasy *The Thief of Baghdad* (1939). He later became associated with films set in Africa, such as *Simba* (1955). Two of Martins's films, *Where No Vultures Fly* (1951) and *Sammy Goes South* (1963), were granted Royal Command Performances. A career on the London stage included *The Heart of the Matter* (1953). In 1954 he starred in *Cry the Beloved Country*, a political protest play about South Africa, in St Martin-in-the-Fields, Trafalgar Square, later starring in the British television version (1958). In 1970 Martins was granted Honorary Life Membership of Equity. He retired to Nigeria in the early 1980s where he died in 1986, receiving a state funeral.

Uzo Egonu, artist, printmaker and art historian. He came to Britain in 1945 at the age of thirteen, and in his later career was recognized as one of the most significant Black artists in Europe. He worked in studios in Hampstead and Wembley; his art has won major prizes and is displayed in the Victoria and Albert Museum, in the Bradford City Art Gallery, and in galleries and museums across the world. The esteem with which Egonu was regarded internationally was reflected in his appointment by UNESCO as Honorary Counsellor for life in 1983. Egonu studied European and Nigerian art history and observed that the Nok civilization of the ninth century BC was regarded as 'classical' until Europeans discovered it had been created by Africans and not the ancient Greeks; then it was redefined as 'primitive'. In this instance, and throughout his life, Egonu fought against restrictive categorization of artists of African origin within modern art. Egonu died in 1996.

Ronald Moody, one of Britain's outstanding post-Second World War sculptors. Moody was born in Jamaica in 1900 and came to England in 1923 to study dentistry at King's College, London. But he was inspired by Egyptian artefacts at the British Museum and turned to sculpture. He later settled in Paris and exhibited his bronzes and carvings there in 1937. When Germany invaded France in 1940 he fled to England where he worked as a dentist in a public health department and took part in London's civil defence. After the war he was a regular exhibitor at the Royal Academy. In 1963 he was commissioned by the Jamaican government to produce a sculpture of the Savacou bird of Carib mythology. One of his sculptures now stands in the Department of Culture, Media and Sport, and has been adopted as a logo by the Caribbean Artists' Movement and by the Caribbean University Press. Based in London, in later life he received Jamaica's Musgrave Gold Medal (1978) for contributions to culture, and the Minority Rights Award for contributions to sculpture in Britain. Moody died in 1984. The picture shows him working on the wood carving 'Three Heads' which is now exhibited at the Nehru Memorial Museum in Delhi.

Pete Badejo in *Ebo Iye, Ritual for Survival* (1988–9). Badejo is one of the leading Black choreographers in Britain. He is also a story-teller, a master musician, a singer and an accomplished actor–director. Born in 1947, Badejo studied dance and choreography both in Nigeria and at the London School of Contemporary Arts (1971). His performances and workshops have attracted large audiences from Britain and abroad. They range from the comic, such as *The Gods Are Not to Blame* (1989–90), to the classical, such as *Medea* (1991): all exhibit warmth, irony, humour and physical authority. Badejo established Badejo Arts in London in 1993 to 'develop African performing arts as a progressive, contemporary form which is both creative and relevant to people's lives and experiences in Britain today'. Peter Badejo is a board member of LIFT, the organization responsible for London's largest performing arts festival; he is also a member of the Arts Council of England's dance panel.

The seamstress Esther Bruce (left), with her stepmother and father. Esther Bruce created gowns for many famous women; Elisabeth Welch is wearing one of her creations in the photograph opposite. Esther was born in Fulham in 1912 to a Scottish mother, Edith Brooks, and a Guianan father, Joseph Bruce. After the death of her mother, she was taught to sew by her stepmother, Jeanie Edwards, who had emigrated to England from British Guiana. After leaving school at the age of fifteen, Esther Bruce worked for the dressmaker Madam Polly and Barkers of Kensington, being sacked from the latter in 1931 because of her colour.

From 1935 to 1941 Esther Bruce worked for Mary Taylor in Chelsea, dressmaker to the rich and famous. Her father Joseph died in London during the Blitz and Esther moved in with neighbour and family friend, Granny Johnson, the matriarch of Dieppe Street (right). In 1941 Esther began war work in the linen room at the Brompton Hospital, where she was to stay for fourteen years, leaving in 1956 to make curtains in Fulham. She retired in 1972, but boredom brought her out of retirement to work for another curtain manufacturer in Battersea. Poor eyesight forced her to retire finally at seventy-four. Esther Bruce died in 1994, having published her autobiography, *Aunt Esther's Story*, three years earlier.

Elisabeth Welch, a prominent member of London's theatrical community since the 1930s, as both a singer and actress, in radio, film, television and theatre. In 1936 she starred with Paul Robeson in the film *Song of Freedom*. *Live from Alexandra Palace*, in the same year, made her one of the first British television stars. She was born in New York in 1909. Maternal encouragement led Welch to join the Europe-bound Americans of the 1920s. In the craze for musical revues, Elisabeth Welch joined Florence Mill's Blackbirds in 1928, in Paris. Her London debut was at the Leicester Square Theatre, in 1933, in *Dark Doings*, introducing the song 'Stormy Weather'. Elisabeth Welch was one of the first Black people to have her own BBC radio series, *Soft Lights and Sweet Music*, as early as 1934, which made her a household name in Britain. She has performed at some of the most prestigious theatrical venues in London and has appeared in two Royal Variety performances (1979 and 1985). Her long list of credits for television drama culminated in a Variety Club of Great Britain Award for services to British entertainment in 1988.

Earl Cameron, is a British actor of screen, stage, television and radio. He played a leading role as a London GP in *Sapphire* (1959). A ground-breaking detective film dealing with racial attitudes in Britain, and including some of the leading Black British actors and actresses of the 1950s, *Sapphire* was a critical and box office success in both the UK and America. Earl Cameron was born in Bermuda in 1925. He joined the British Merchant Navy and came to London to live in 1939. His cinema début, also considered a classic, was *Pool of London* (1950). His other films have included Graham Greene's *Heart of the Matter* (1953), *Simba* (1955), *Accused* (1957), *Flame in the Streets* (1961) (above), *Term of Trial* (1962), *Thunderball* (1965), *Battle Beneath the Earth* (1968) and *The Revolutionary* (1979). Cameron's performances have spanned all film genres from action to science fiction to social realism, and he has played opposite noted international actors, such as Sidney Poitier and Laurence Olivier. His work in several popular television series such as *Dixon of Dock Green*, *Emergency Ward 10* and *Danger Man* did much to increase the visibility of Black actors on British television. He settled briefly in New Zealand in the late 1980s, but later returned to London to work in the West End and for television. Cameron's more recent appearances include *Lovejoy* (1995) and *The Great Kandinski*.

Rudolph Walker, the TV and stage actor, as a young actor in the 1960s. Born in Trinidad in 1940, Walker arrived in London 1960, where he worked as a compositor in the printing trade by day, while at night he studied drama at the City Literary Institute. After a series of small parts in TV, film and theatre his big break came with the TV comedy *Love Thy Neighbour*, which ran for five years and earned him the TV Personality of the Year Award from the Variety Club of Great Britain in 1972. One of Britain's most popular television comedies, *Love Thy Neighbour* dealt with a Black family's encounter with racism in a White suburb. *Love Thy Neighbour* used comedy to look at racism in modern Britain, which until then had only been dealt with in highbrow drama or worthy documentary, if at all. More recently he starred as PC Gladstone in *The Thin Blue Line*. He has also enjoyed a successful West End stage career, with leading roles in *The Tempest* and *Othello*. In 1992 Walker was presented with the Scarlet Ibis Award for 'outstanding and meritorious service' by the Trinidad and Tobago High Commission.

Nina Baden-Semper, actress of television, stage and film, was born in Le Brea, Trinidad, and came to Britain in 1965 to study nursing at the Hammersmith Hospital where she became an SRN and SCM. Baden-Semper and her co-star Rudolph Walker in the popular comedy, *Love Thy Neighbour*, were the first Black actors to star in a major television series. She became a style and cultural icon in the 1970s. In 1973 she was awarded ITV Joint Television Personality Award by the Variety Club of Great Britain, and Outstanding Female Personality of the Year PYE TV Award. She appeared on *This Is Your Life* (1975) and was presented with the Scarlet Ibis Award for Outstanding and Meritorious Service by the Trinidad and Tobago government (1990).

Film-maker Menelik Shabazz working on the television documentary *Breaking Point* in 1978. Shabazz was born in 1954 in St John, Barbados, and has lived in London since the age of five. He attended the London International Film School (1974–6) and has worked as an independent film-maker since. In 1980 with his first feature-length film *Burning an Illusion*, which he both wrote and directed, Shabazz forged new traditions in British Black film-making. *Burning an Illusion*, an attempt to capture the Black urban experience, is a tale of the pressure endured by the young British-born Black community. He has completed many other projects including *Catch a Fire*, a drama documentary made for the BBC.

Cassie McFarlane and Victor Romero Evans in *Burning an Illusion* 1981.

Cynthia Moody directing an advertisement for Beecham's, 1964–5. Cynthia Moody's career charts the early involvement of Black British women as film-makers. She founded her own production and post-production companies. She has also been an early exponent of international TV and film advertising. Born in 1923, Moody trained at the Shell Film Unit and was a cine operator in the WRNS during the Second World War. After the war, she trained as a film editor, dialogue writer and dubbing editor, and went on to produce films for British Films Ltd, the Central Office for Information and the Children's Film Foundation; she also worked with Jacques Tati in Paris on *Monsieur Hulot's Holiday*. Her work has won many awards. She is now the curator of the Ronald Moody Archive in Bristol.

The Ital Lions (Brinsley Forde, Brian Bovell, Victor Romero Evans, Trevor Laird and David N. Haynes) with Ronnie (Karl Howman, centre) in *Babylon*. *Babylon*, a film made by Franco Rosso in 1980, marked the coming of age of Black London youth and was a milestone in their cultural resistance against social injustice. The film describes the experiences of a young Londoner torn between the two worlds of low-paid employment as a mechanic and evening work as a DJ improvising lyrics over reggae sound-tracks at a night-club. The counter-culture of the latter is portrayed as both an escape from the ghetto and a coming to terms with an emergent Black self-identity. The film's sound-track featured some of the finest exponents of London's reggae scene, and challenged the narrow perception of this music. Reggae stars also took leading acting roles, such as the members of the group Aswad. *Babylon* today stands as a social document of Black London youth and culture in the 1980s, commenting as it does on the crumbling inner city, police harassment and contemporary music and dance.

Brinsley Forde, actor and singer with leading reggae band Aswad. He was a child star of the 1960s children's television series, *The Double Deckers*.

Samuel Coleridge-Taylor, composer of the English choral orchestral work *Hiawatha's Wedding Feast*. Sales of sheet music show this was the most popular choral orchestral piece between 1898 and 1912. Coleridge-Taylor was considered by Edward Elgar, as well as by Sir George Grove, his Principal at the Royal College of Music, to be one of the most outstanding British musicians and composers of his generation. Born in Holborn in 1875, he moved to Croydon, where he was an early supporter of Pan-Africanism, a London-born movement to secure civil and political rights for Africans throughout the world. Coleridge-Taylor and John Archer (*see* p. 65) were voted onto the executive committee of the Pan-Africanist Conference that they organized in Westminster Town Hall in 1900. Coleridge-Taylor's popularity as a musician led to an invitation to the White House by President Theodore Roosevelt, and to his being championed by America's Black community. He became Professor of Composition at the Trinity College of Music in 1903 and at the Guildhall School of Music in 1910. He died in 1912.

Born in British Guiana in 1907, Rudolph Dunbar was trained at the Institute of Musical Art, Juliard School, New York (1919). Coming to Europe in 1928, Dunbar studied journalism and music at the University of Paris and Conservatory of Music; he also attended conservatories in Leipzig and Vienna to study conducting, composition and the clarinet.

In 1936 Dunbar was commissioned to act as roving reporter for the Associated Negro Press to cover the Italian invasion of Ethiopia. On 26 April 1942, Dunbar led the London Philharmonic Orchestra, at the Royal Albert Hall, to raise funds for persons of African descent in the Allied fighting forces. He was appointed as an accredited war correspondent in the Second World War and achieved the distinction of covering the Normandy Invasion, the invasion of Paris and the fall of Berlin. He is shown here with Lady Pitt.

Dunbar conducted classical concerts in both Paris and Berlin, the orchestras of the Paris Conservatoire, the National Symphony of Paris and the Berlin Philharmonic Orchestra. But London had always been the base for his international career. In his early career he led a series of jazz orchestras, with residencies at several London restaurants, such as the Cossack, to finance his classical studies. In the mid-1920s he accompanied performers such as Florence Mills and Josephine Baker on their European tours. He formed his own clarinet school and wrote the first ever treatise on the clarinet in 1939; his training manuals for the clarinet became classics for aspiring clarinet players. Rudolph Dunbar died in 1988.

Ian Hall at the organ of Westminster Central Hall, at a fundraising recital for the Commonwealth, 1993. Born in Guyana in 1940, and nephew of the Black British conductor Rudolph Dunbar (*see* pp. 24–5), Hall has become a leading light in church and classical music in London since the 1960s, when he was Assistant Organist at St Martin-in-the-Fields and Deputy Organist and Chorister at Southwark Cathedral. He was appointed Director of Music to the Inner London Education Authority in 1966, and later became Conductor and Director of Music both of the London University Church of Christ the King and of the University of London Choir. In 1970 he founded the Bloomsbury International Society for the propagation of racial harmony through music, which grew out of a multicultural festival to celebrate United Nations Human Rights Day. In 1996 Hall conducted his own work, *Vivat Pax*, in New York before assembled world leaders as part of the United Nations fiftieth anniversary celebrations. In 1997 he was Master of Ceremonies for the Commonwealth Summit in Edinburgh.

Tunde Jegede, composer and musician of classical African and Western music. Born in 1972, Jegede began studying the kora, the African harp-lute, when he was six; when he was seven he joined the Purcell School of Music in London, and in 1980 he took up a musical apprenticeship in the Gambia, a first for a British musician. On his return he joined the Guildhall School of Music and Drama; before he left in 1992 he was at the heart of a musical and cultural revolution that re-evaluated the African classical music tradition. He traced the African roots of Western classical music to the Moorish invasion of Spain and the rebab (or rebec), from which the modern violin has evolved. Jegede formed the African Classical Music Ensemble in 1991; he has also written and performed music for dance companies, theatre and film, and written several books about African music. He thus continues to ensure that the African musical traditions find expression in the West.

The singer-songwriter Gabrielle. Gabrielle served her apprenticeship on the night club circuit, singing cover versions of Motown classics. The anthem 'Dreams' came out of this period, and describes her dejection at the elusiveness of professional success. This, however, made chart history by going straight in at Number 2, the highest entry for a debut artist at the time. Her debut album 'Find Your Way' sold almost one million copies when it was released in 1993. Her second album, 'Gabrielle', was released in 1995. It included the hit single 'Give Me a Little More Time', and led to a new creative direction in producing for the Boilerhouse Boys.

Baron Leary Constantine of Maraval and Nelson (right) with the Trinidadian premier Sir Eric Williams, 1962. Lear
Nicholas Constantine was born on a cocoa estate in Trinidad in 1901. He came to London in 1923 and became
phenomenal cricketing success as batsman, fast bowler and fielder. In 1928 he took 100 wickets and scored 1,000 runs
and was invited to settle in Britain. In the 1930s he became a spokesperson for the Black community, negotiating wit
employers and the trade unions to place Black workers in industry during the Second World War. As Captain of the Wes
Indies cricket team against England at Lords in 1943 he sued the manageress of the Imperial Hotel, Russell Square, fo
breach of contract in refusing accommodation to Constantine and his family because of their colour. He was awarded a
MBE in 1945, and went on to serve as Minister of Transport and the Trinidad and Tobago High Commissioner to Grea
Britain. Knighted in 1962, Constantine was made a life peer in 1969. He died in 1971.

Harold Ernest Moody as Mayor of Auckland, New Zealand. Moody was born in Peckham in 1915, the son of the Black community leader and Congregationalist minister Harold Moody (*see* p. 47). He qualified as a doctor in 1941, serving as a commissioned officer and army doctor on troop ships in many theatres of war, and then in India, before returning to the family practice in Peckham. In 1948 he represented Britain in the shot-put and discus at the Olympic Games, held at Wembley Stadium. He went on the win gold medals for these events at the 1950 Empire Games. He settled in New Zealand in 1951, where he became a popular and active member of the Auckland community, serving as mayor from 1967 to 1971. He died in 1986.

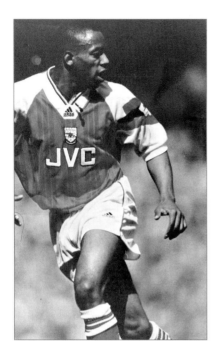

Born in Woolwich in 1963, Ian Wright started out in non-league football before joining Crystal Palace. He then spent seven years at Arsenal before moving on to West Ham United and picked up England honours on the way.

Lennox Lewis (right) was born in West Ham, East London in 1965. He is the first Briton to hold a world heavyweight championship title since Bob Fitzsimmons 100 years ago. Yet in 1988 when Lennox Lewis won the Olympic super-heavyweight title, in Seoul, against Riddick Bowe, he was wearing the Canadian vest of his adopted home. When South London pub owner Frank Malone heard he was a Londoner by birth, he set about the task of reclaiming this sportsman and chess player for Britain. With an estimated fortune of £45 million, Lewis has been called 'the richest sportsman in Europe', a title he rejects, preferring to live a relatively modest lifestyle, concentrating on his boxing career and his biggest single outlay, The Lennox Lewis College, in East London (a private secondary school for disadvantaged children of African Caribbean origin). He won the WBC title in 1992, lost it in 1994, and won it back in 1997. He is pictured here with Ian Wright (left).

CHAPTER TWO

MILITARY

In 1775, Virginia's Royal Governor, Lord Dunmore, promised to 'arm my own negroes and receive all others that shall come to me who I shall call free'. This was the promise which encouraged thousands of Black loyalists, who consisted of both those who had been enslaved and freemen, to join the British side in the American War of Independence. When the British retreated, they evacuated 14,000 Black soldiers from Savannah, Charleston and New York, many of whom came to England, swelling the Black population of London. While some were able to continue their trades, such as cookshop owners and shoemakers, the vast majority joined the London poor as beggars and street musicians, being deprived of even Army back pay and compensation for war injuries, and denied work due to prejudice.

The Navy too had been a regular employer of Black Londoners and their relatives, many of whom settled in parts of the capital with naval or military connections. Since the fifteenth century, London ships had set sail for Africa for the purposes of trade, a policy officially sanctioned by the creation of Royal Charter companies, such as the Royal Africa Company (1670). Later the British slave trade and west African commodities funded the building of a modern Navy, and the emergence of British naval might. The Navy ensured the passage of African peoples and cargo, and the Army facilitated conquest of their territory and the maintenance of imperial control.

English regiments regularly served in the West Indies from the seventeenth century onwards, often returning to London with West Indian soldiers, servants, slaves and musicians. With the abolition of the slave trade in 1807, London became the home of thousands of Black people. By this time it had long-established direct links with ports throughout Africa and the West Indies.

This relationship between the major port of London and Africa and the West Indies was to continue with the trade in commodities, which replaced the slave trade. Thus it was that many descendants of the enslaved Africans who peopled the factory islands of West Indies, and descendants of free Africans involved in trade, diplomacy and study, docked in London's ports as soldiers, sailors and adventurers. By the time of the First and Second World Wars, the link between metropolitan London and Empire ensured the free flow of human capital from the Empire to London.

During the Second World War women were to serve in a broader capacity than in previous generations, as military nurses and doctors, in the ATS, the WAAF and the Red Cross, and to work in munitions factories. Colonel Christine Moody had the distinction of becoming one of the first Black women officers in the British Army in 1940, going on to become a pioneer in the early years of the United Nations World Health Organization, on regional health projects in West Africa and the Caribbean.

Many African and Caribbean men and women came to London on active service in the Army, Navy and Air Force. Many met and married Black Londoners from families that had settled under previous waves of immigration. And many who came to London in the postwar wave of immigration had previously come to London as servicemen and women and war-workers.

Despite the historical links of Black Londoners to the armed services, the experience of people like Richard Sykes, Britain's first Black Guardsman, demonstrates that little has changed in their discriminatory treatment. Despite a well-publicized arrival, his military career was ended by a campaign of racial harassment.

Donald Adolphus Brown, sailor. Brown was born in 1874 at Woolwich to an English woman and a Jamaican Petty Officer in the Royal Navy. He was one of the many Black children educated at the Royal Hospital School in the nineteenth century; he then served as a sailor in the Merchant Navy, before becoming foreman at Woolwich Arsenal. He was awarded the Edward Medal for bravery in 1921 after he put out a fire in an explosives store at great risk to his life. Brown married the noted Suffragette Eliza Adelaide Knight. He died in 1949.

West India Regiment, *c.* 1919. Rules on alien enlistment are revealing about the perception of Black people as falling int
a unique category, neither alien nor British. Black people were quite simply regarded as an 'exception'. While th
proportion of aliens within a regiment was not supposed to exceed one in fifty, this rule was not applied in relation t
Black men and women. Without this exception, the British Army in Africa and the Caribbean could not have maintaine
the Empire.

    This photograph shows the British West India Regiment on the eve of travel to Italy. Many of these men were later t
become disillusioned with London, where they stopped on the way home, by a spate of anti-Black riots which took place i
the capital. The rioting was in response to the increased Black presence due to military demobilization of African and Wes
Indian troops after the war. Black troops were also denied participation in the victory celebrations, referred to as the Peac
March, on 19 July 1919. Riots took place in Stepney, Limehouse and West India Dock Road with assaults on Blac
Londoners and soldiers and damage to their property.

    The history of colonial troops in British Army began long before the beginning of the Second World War. The coronatio
of Edward VII in 1902 provided a unique opportunity for a show of imperial military strength. In June, therefor
Alexandra Palace was turned into a barracks and the grounds into a tented camp for 2,500 colonial troops. Because th
coronation was delayed due to Edward's illness, the troops stayed for the entire summer. The trustees of the palac
capitalized on the camp as a tourist attraction by organizing a review by the Duke of Connaught and by inviting the troop
to attend the London Coronation Cup race meeting in July. On August Bank Holiday over 100,000 Londoners flocked t
Alexandra Palace to view the spectacle of troops from every colonial regiment from the West Indies to the Sudan. The ai
was to demonstrate living proof of the reach of Empire. Today, Dr Bernie Grant, the Black MP for Tottenham, is a truste
of Alexandra Palace.

Constance Goodridge-Mark (left) on her way to work, Jamaica, 1944, and (right) in the 1980s. Born Constance Mcdonald in Kingston, Jamaica, in 1923, she joined the British Army in 1943, serving in the Auxiliary Territorial Service, the Women's Royal Army Corps and Queen Alexandra's Royal Army Nursing Corps before becoming Senior Medical Secretary in the Royal Army Medical Corps for ten years, working in the North Caribbean. She joined her husband, a professional cricketer, in Shepherd's Bush in 1954, and became medical secretary to some of London's most distinguished specialists, including Sir John Peel, the Queen's Gynaecologist. Goodridge-Mark became Project Officer for the British Council for Aid to Refugees in the 1980s, being responsible for the settlement of the Vietnam 'boat people' in Britain. She plays a leading role in several national and local organizations, such as the Commission for Racial Equality, and has founded several organizations of her own, such as the Friends of Mary Seacole Memorial Association (1986). She was awarded the British Empire Medal for services to the community in 1992.

King George VI and Queen Elizabeth, with Flight Lieutenant De Souza from Jamaica and the Princesses Elizabeth and Margaret, inspecting a parade of West Indians on VE Day, May 1945.

Colonel Charles Arundel Moody. Born in Peckham in 1917, Moody became the first Black officer in the British Army during the Second World War when he joined the Queen's Own Royal West Kent Regiment in 1940. His father, Dr Harold Moody (see p. 47), who was President of the League of Coloured Peoples, had protested to the Colonial Secretary about the 'colour bar' (accepted discriminatory practice) in the armed services; as a result the government relaxed the rules regarding voluntary enlistment and emergency commissions. Charles Moody served in the Infantry and the Artillery in England and Africa, then in Italy and finally in Egypt, where he became a Major in 1945. At the end of the war he returned to Jamaica with B Company of the Caribbean Regiment, settling there for the next forty years. Moody became a Colonel in 1961, and was awarded an OBE in 1966 as the first Commanding Officer of the Jamaican Territorial Army.

Group Captain Osborne, OBE. Osborne was a Coastal Command navigator before becoming a member of the Anglo-German Technical Commission, engaged in the training and re-supply of the German Air Force. He was also responsible for introducing the RAF's computerized supply system into the main depots. In 1969 he was awarded an OBE for his work in maintenance command.

During the Second World War Black servicemen and women were often distributed throughout the country, on different bases and in different branches of the armed services, which led to the isolation of servicemen when they retired. To rectify this situation, Allan Kelly, Hector Watson and Arnaud Horner founded the West Indian Ex-Servicemen's (and Women's) Association in 1971, which provided a single venue for Black people who had served in the forces to socialize and share experiences and later to educate the community at large on the historical role of West Indian servicemen and women. This is the earliest available photograph of the founders of the association taken in 1971. Left to right: Anthony Goddard, Michael Armand, Mr Adam, Allan Kelly, Mr Clarke, Neil Flanigan.

Officers and members of the West Indian Ex-Servicemen's (and Women's) Association in their Clapham premises. Front, left to right: R. Webb, N. Flanigan, S. King (Mayor of Southwark), Hector Watson, L. Phillpotts. Back, left to right: V. Hunte, Mr Bravo, A. Armstrong, Mr Aiken. One of the more recent highlights of the organization's history was when the Governor-General of Jamaica and the President of Jamaica, Trinidad and Tobago, together with distinguished politicians and high commissioners from all over the Caribbean, joined the association in commemorating the fiftieth anniversary of VJ Day.

Allan Kelly. Born in 1918, Kelly joined the RAF in Jamaica and came to Britain in 1944.

After the war Allan Kelly became a civil servant, retiring in 1984 after forty years' continuous government service. He is pictured on the left of the photograph above, which was taken in 1997 at the passing out parade for Jamaican servicemen at Sandhurst, with His Excellency Mr Haven, Jamaican High Commissioner to London, and Mr Watson, co-founder of the West Indian Ex-Servicemen's (and Women's) Association. A tireless community activist, he was a leading patron and founder-member of a host of organizations, including the West Indian Ex-Servicemen's (and Women's) Association and Paddington Churches Housing Association, one of the largest housing associations in London. He was Ward Secretary and Ward Vice-Chairman of the Conservative Party and served on various other committees, including the Notting Hill Carnival Police Committee and the Central London branch of the Royal Air Force Association. He has the distinction of having a block of flats in Westbourne Park named after him. Allan Kelly died in 1998 and his funeral service is pictured below.

Hector Watson with his wife Edithna, 1970s. Born in 1924 in St Catherine, Jamaica, Watson joined the RAF in Jamaica in 1943 and was sent to Britain in the same year. As well as serving in Bomber Command, he became part of the secret convoy of lorry drivers who drove radar equipment to and from factories concealed in the Welsh mountains. In 1960 he established Flywheel and Co., Lambeth Hill, one of the first Black-owned haulage transport companies in Britain. Flywheel and Co. brought coal from the Midlands to powerhouses in London on 5 ton lorries, using techniques later incorporated into all haulage transport design. Watson's technical expertise was later sought by the Transport Section of the Home Office, where he oversaw the roadworthiness of diplomatic cars for UK and overseas service. Watson was a founder member of the West Indian Ex-Servicemen's (and Women's) Association and President of the Royal British Legion, Brixton and Stockwell. He received an award for services to the community from the Jamaican High Commission.

Neil Flanigan in RAF uniform. Born in Jamaica in 1924, Flanigan joined the RAF during the Second World War and came to Britain in 1944. After the war he worked for many years as an engineer for major British airlines, but in 1985 he retrained as an accountant. He has been involved in many community committees and projects, including serving for eleven years on the Police Consultative Committee, Lambeth. He has also been an active member and officer of the West Indian Ex-Servicemen (and Women's) Association. In 1993 Flanigan became an Independent Person, under the Children's Act, for the County of Hampshire, and two years later was made a member of the Independent Persons Committee for Lambeth; in the 1990s he has also sat on a host of committees for the High Commission of Jamaica.

Laurie Phillpotts, the current Information Officer of the West Indian Ex-Servicemen's (and Women's) Association. In this capacity he has developed the educational resources of the organization that relate to the West Indian and African contribution to the British at war and in peacetime.

Laurie Phillpotts has contributed to many exhibitions, including 'Living Memory' (1987), which was shown at the Gunnersbury Park Museum and County Hall.

Richard Sykes, Britain's first Black Guardsman, at his passing out parade, Pirbright, Surrey, 1987. In 1997 a campaign was launched by the Ministry of Defence to recruit Black Londoners to the armed services. Despite the historical linkages of Black Londoners to the armed services, the experience of people like Richard Sykes, who left the service due to racial harassment, demonstrates that little has changed in discriminatory treatment of Black people in the military. Modern Black Londoners are less prepared to tolerate racial harassment, wherever they may be employed.

CHAPTER THREE

HEALTH & WELFARE

The National Health Service has been one of the largest employers of Black people in the twentieth century, and as a consequence is a major repository of the history of Black Londoners. However, few are aware of the pivotal contributions in its earliest phases of evolution of health workers and care-givers such as Dr George Rice, Dr Harold Moody and Colonel Christine Moody.

Dr Rice took the pioneering work of Joseph Lister, 'the father of antiseptic', out of the operating theatre and turned it into a matter of general public health, in hospitals and schools in South London and surrounding districts.

During his lifetime, Dr Harold Moody did much to change the employment patterns of Black women within the National Health Service by challenging the 'colour bar' in their employment as nurses in British hospitals in the 1940s. Also, as a father he supported the education of his daughters in the fields of education and medicine, inspiring his daughter Christine to follow in his footsteps and beyond. Dr Harold Moody's experiences of hardship and racial discrimination within the medical profession and society at large led him to found the League of Coloured Peoples in 1931, one of the first effective Black pressure groups in Britain. When asked what he died from, family friend Dr Alex Buxton-Thomas, who performed the autopsy, said 'overwork'.

Christine Moody went on to make history in her own right. As a trailblazer in the early days of the World Health Organization, she led many of the earliest development and health programmes in Africa, the West Indies, the Far East and South America. Not bad going for a Peckham GP!

Modern techniques in primary care and specialist treatments now make it possible for people to survive who would not have done so decades ago. These changes are not dependent upon a single invention or revelation, but on many techniques developed over time by health care workers, sharing knowledge and observations which then become common practice. Black Londoners have been ever-present where such advances have been made, and directly and indirectly may lay claim to many innovations in medicine, nursing and public health.

Dr George Rice, who extended antiseptic research to South London hospitals and schools.

Dr Rice was born in 1848, the son of freed slaves. He settled in Plumstead, South London, after studying medicine under Dr Lister at Edinburgh Royal Infirmary; Lister was famous for his work in antiseptic treatment in surgery. Rice was appointed Superintendent of Woolwich Union Infirmary in 1877, and in 1884 he was selected out of eighty-four candidates as Resident Medical Officer of the Sutton District Schools. From 1886 to 1917 Rice did some trailblazing research into epilepsy at Belmont Workhouse. In the group photograph of Belmont staff (above), Dr Rice is seated second from the right, second row. He died in 1935.

Surgeon Major J.B. Africanus Horton MD (Edinburgh), an eminent nineteenth-century Igbo physician, political scientist and banker in British Army Uniform.

Audrey McCracken, midwife, teacher and specialist
in primary care and health promotion. Born in
Barbados to a seamstress and a police sergeant in
1936, she came to England to study nursing at
Hillingdon Hospital in 1959. After training as a
midwife in Birmingham and London, she taught
midwifery at Edgware Hospital and Bushy
Maternity Hospital from 1977 to 1982. During this
period she did pioneering research into Special
Care Baby Units under Dr Balthorp, and in the
1980s she was one of the first Black professionals
involved with haemoglobinopathy research and
sufferer-counselling at the Central Middlesex
Hospital. She also co-ordinated the primary care
and health promotion work of eight surgeries in
Harrow and Brent, winning a health promotion
award in 1991. Nurse McCracken became a Master
of Science at Brunel University in 1995. She
continues to serve on the committee of the Clinical
Research Nurses Association.

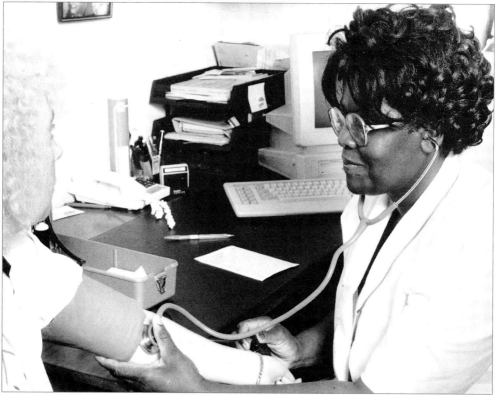

Dr Harold Moody, doctor, Congregationalist minister, community leader and civil rights activist. Born in 1882, the son of a druggist, Moody came to England in 1904 to study medicine at King's College, London. He qualified in 1910, having won several academic awards. Denied the post of Medical Officer to the Camberwell Board of Guardians because of open racism, he went on to run surgeries in South London: Queen's Road, Peckham, King's Grove, Pepys Hill and New Cross Gate. Moody's early experiences of hardship and racial discrimination led him to found, with Stella Thomas and others, the League of Coloured Peoples in 1931. Moody was responsible for enabling the first Black nurse to train in Britain and the first Black officer to join the British Army. He died in 1947.

Colonel Christine Moody, a pioneer in the early years of the United Nations World Health Organization (WHO). She was born in South London in 1914, the daughter of the Black community leader Harold Moody (*see* p. 47). After qualifying as member of the Royal College of Surgeons in 1938 she joined her father's practices in South London.

Christine Moody became an officer in the Royal Army Medical Corps early in the Second World War, shortly after her brother Charles had become the first Black officer in the British Army (*see* p. 36). In 1944 she was put in charge of the British Military Hospital in Ambala, Punjab, and after the war she spent ten years in Ghana as Senior Medical Officer with the Ministry of Health, developing maternity, paediatric and public health projects throughout the country.

Colonel Christine Moody went on to act as consultant in development and primary care to the WHO and the World Bank, as health adviser to the Philippines and as Chief Medical Officer for Public Health in Jamaica. She was made Commander of the Order of Distinction, Jamaica, in 1988.

Mrs Kura King-Okokon, nurse, midwife and voluntary sector worker. Kura King-Okokon came to London in December 1958 as a registered general nurse from Barbados to pursue a career in nursing, arriving at Paddington from the SS *Antilles* boat-train. She first lived in Stoke Newington, and subsequently married the late Dr C.O.I. Okokon, a Nigerian consultant at the West Middlesex Hospital. They raised three daughters – a scientist, a teacher and a social policy researcher. Mrs King-Okokon later became the first female co-ordinator of the WISE (West Indian Self-Effort) Project. The black voluntary sector has done much to redefine statutory provision in education, health and senior citizens' care, often addressing unmet needs, and mediating between care agencies and the Black community. Without the Black voluntary sector these agencies would be less sensitive to the needs of London's multi-cultural communities. For instance, the WISE Project's Supplementary School emerged in response to Black parents, who demanded action when the education system was failing their children; and before its Luncheon Club, there was little recognition of the dietary needs of African-Caribbean senior citizens in Brent, London's most ethnically diverse borough.

Mrs King-Okokon has served on the Education Committee Advisory Group to the Barbados High Commission, London, since 1996.

Shirlene Rudder MBE, specialist genetic health visitor for the North West Thames Region. Born in Barbados in 1946, Rudder emigrated to the UK when she was eighteen, and trained as a nurse and midwife, becoming a health visitor in 1972 and a health visitor fieldwork teacher two years later. She settled in Kenton, north-west London, and set up the Harlesden branch of the Sickle-Cell Society in 1979 – sickle-cell amaemia is a disease that primarily affects people of African descent – and became increasingly involved in genetics. As a specialist genetic health visitor, she is responsible for the testing and counselling of families at risk of sickle-cell anaemia, cystic fibrosis, Down's syndrome and muscular dystrophy. Rudder was made an MBE in 1995 for her work for the Genetic Service.

Elizabeth Okokon, Senior Clinical Biochemist at King's College Hospital. Born in Wales in 1964 to a Nigerian father and a Barbadian mother, Okokon feels that she can truly define herself as Afro-Caribbean. She has lived in London since the age of three, attending school in Harrow. The racism and sexism she experienced nearly prevented her from pursuing her chosen career; she is, as a result, a member of Southwark Council's Black Mentor Scheme, where Black professionals provide guidance to teenagers to encourage them to fulfil their educational potential. She sat her MSc Part I exam a week before giving birth to her son, Kwame, and had a daughter in time for her graduation ceremony, while managing a laboratory at the same time. From 1989 to 1995 Elizabeth ran the Diagnostic Research Unit in the Academic Department of Obstetrics and Gynaecology, King's College, where she published research on infertility, the menopause and hormone replacement therapy. She is now working towards a PhD into the onset of puberty in girls.

CHAPTER FOUR

TRADE, INDUSTRY & ENTERPRISE

WHO PUT THE OIL IN THE LAMP?

That London emerged as a premier port is due substantially to the economic contributions of Africans and West Indians. Trade in West African commodities and the advent of the slave trade facilitated vast accumulations of wealth and propelled the growth of the British Empire and the Industrial Revolution. So substantial was the wealth generated and accumulated that the City of London, as a global financial centre, still trades on its residue.

Between them, Africa and the Caribbean put the wax in the candle, the oil in the lamp, the sugar in the tea, the copper in the kettles, the rum on the table, the fruit in the basket, the cotton on the back, the diamond on the fingers, the gold in the pocket and, quite literally, kept the wheels of the Industrial Revolution turning through industrial lubricants.

The men and women of sugar and banking funded an empire to whose greater glory such London landmarks were created as the British Museum and the Victoria & Albert Museum, which showed off the spoils of imperial conquest. The core of National Gallery's collection was based on pictures acquired by John Julius Angerstein, the famous Lloyd's underwriter who was associated with the slave trade. So entrenched with sugar and slavery in the Caribbean were London's banking interests that the Bank of England was referred to as 'The Bank of the West Indies'.

ENTERPRISE AS SELF-EMPOWERMENT AND EMANCIPATION

British history is not the comfort zone which some might hope to retreat into. London's economic structures have also benefited from the waves of Black immigration over centuries, in addition to the wealth of labour and resources extracted through a global empire. The relationship between enterprise and slavery has always been a complex one.

Enterprise can make a freeman out of a slave or a slave out of the free. Economic emancipation often preceded freedom under slavery: among the enslaved, some men and women were able to buy their freedom, while at the same time the profitability of the slave economy led to its continuance over centuries. Sadly, generations of Black Londoners have learned that the fact of personal freedom does not always guarantee economic freedom. Without the means or opportunity to pursue a trade or access employment, they were well represented among the beggars and the poor of London.

However, some were fortunate and many Black Londoners were to become well-known local traders: Ignatius Sancho and his wife Anne ran a grocer's store in Charles Street, Westminster; Robert Wedderburn and William Cuffay were tailors; other trades in which Black Londoners took an active role were as publicans, publishers, cookshop owners, entertainers, carpenters and blacksmiths.

TRADING KINGS AND QUEENS

The trading power of Africa itself was often diminished by imperial propaganda, which sought to remove the perception of Africans as capable of successful economic activity. Despite the imperialist quest to wrest control of Africa's economic destiny, Europe continued to depend upon the co-operation of West Africa's powerful trading dynasties, without whom access to certain commodities would have been impossible.

Madam Ewa Henshaw, for example, from the royal trading house of Henshaw Town, Old Calabar, Nigeria, was linked to Britain in this way through the export of palm oil. Palm oil was a raw material in the production of soap, margarine, cosmetics, machine grease and candles. Pears soap is a British brand name established world-wide through this vital ingredient.

Here are just some of the descendents of the Black traders, entrepreneurs and industrialists of early twentieth-century London.

A Black tailor, Whitechapel Mission, 1900. Little is known of the Black tailor in this photograph, but Whitechapel in East London is an area long associated with tailoring. The trade attracted many refugees from persecution, especially Russian and Polish Jews.

Madam Ewa Henshaw was from a trading family of Henshaw Town, Old Calabar, Nigeria, which was linked to London through the export of palm oil to Britain – a key raw material in the production of soap, margarine, cosmetics, machine grease and candles. Madam Henshaw was related to King Eyamba V and Archibong I. Her husband, Dr L.E.R. Henshaw OBE, Deputy Director of Medical Services in eastern Nigeria, was descended from an Efik royal house where names were often anglicized to facilitate trade communications.

Sir Edward Asafu Adjaye, the Ghanaian High Commissioner, inspecting logs from the Gliksten concessions in Ghana, with E. Terance Scott, managing director, and R.E. Groves, director, of J. Gliksten & Son, at Stratford Lumber Yard, 1961.

Dudley George Dryden, director of Dyke & Dryden
Ltd, a leading distributor of Black hair and beauty
products in Europe. Born in 1926, Dryden founded
the firm with Len Dyke (*see* below). He has also been
an active community organizer as Vice-Chairman of
the Association of Jamaicans from 1965 to 1975, as a
member of the West Indian Standing Conference
from 1970 to 1980, and as Chair of Hackney
Commission for Racial Equality from 1978 to 1981.
He was awarded an MBE for services to the
community in 1985.

Len Dyke, co-founder of Dyke & Dryden Ltd,
leading distributor of Black hair and beauty products
in Europe.

Dounne Alexander, founder and Chief Executive of Gramma's Ltd, a leading supplier of herbal pepper sources in the UK. Born in 1949, Alexander came to Britain in 1962 to join her parents and sisters in Essex. In 1971 she moved to Forest Gate, East London, but it was from her flat in East Ham that she began Gramma's Ltd in 1987. By 1991 the firm had won national recognition for introducing Black herbal foods to mainstream supermarkets, a success that forced a redefinition of British food culture. In 1991 Gramma's Ltd was forced to liquidate due to its rapid growth rate and the withdrawal of banking support. It was relaunched later that same, however, with new financial backers and a restructuring that has led to an emphasis on the luxury food market and mail order sales. Alexander became Vice-President of London Youth Clubs in 1991 and won a European Women of Achievement Award in 1992.

Joy Nichols, who founded the Nichols Employment Agency with her brother and co-director Lennox Campbell in 1984. The business has grown from a small agency on the Harrow Road, Maida Hill, to expand in the public, private and voluntary sectors, opening two further offices in Peckham High Street and Lee High Road.

Isobel Husbands (née Grant) was born in 1917 and settled in West London in 1955. She bought a succession of houses in London from the 1950s to the 1980s, demonstrating economic independence and shrewd financial management at a time when there was great discrimination in the housing market for Black men, let alone Black women. While working as a cook in a succession of West End restaurants, she developed an interest in dress design, collecting and mixing fabrics. William Husbands, who was born in 1913, worked at Selfridge's in the West End from 1955 to 1980, beginning as a porter and retiring as a supervisor. He believes that he was the first Black man to work at Selfridge's, and in the 1950s when labour was in short supply he acted as a recruiter for the company within the Black community.

Jack Bubuela at the launch of the computer version of the game Nubian Jak which was held at the Cyberia Café, Windmill Street, London. Born Johnny Alexander Bubuela Dodd in 1963, Jack Bubuela was in turn a sound engineer, pop singer and social worker before coming to fame in 1992 as a male model in the 'Face of Interflora' advertisement, the longest-running national advertisement for a single campaign that featured a Black male model. As managing director of KEMCO/MEDIA Concepts he was responsible for creating the Nubian Jak board game in 1994, an Afro-centric trivia game which was unique in bringing facts about Black history and culture to a Black and White audience. Nubian Jak achieved a place in the top ten new games of 1995; the computer version was launched on the Internet by being played simultaneously in the USA, Japan, France and Germany.

Chris Adeshinaro Oluwatoyin Shokoya-Eleshin arriving at Heathrow Airport from Nigeria in 1965 with his parents (above). He settled in Plaistow, East London, at the age of four: the photograph below shows him outside his first London home. He became owner of the most successful building contractors in the UK.

After attending Upton Cross School and Clarkes School, Chris went to Forest Public School, where he survived six racially motivated fights in his first week. Despite this hostile beginning, he excelled academically, socially and on the playing field to become a popular Head of School House. (The photograph above shows him at the Old Boys' dinner in 1981.) A schoolboy county cricketer for Essex,

Shokoya-Eleshin went on to join the MCC as a full playing member; in 1991 he assisted in arranging the first MCC tour of West Africa for twenty years. He taught mathematics at secondary school level before founding Shokoya-Eleshin Construction in 1992 which became one of Britain's largest Black-owned construction companies, with branches in London, Liverpool, Freetown, Lagos and Shagamu. In 1996, the company's £2.3 million housing development in Musgrove Street, Liverpool, was identified by the UK Council to the United Nations as a 'model of good practice', and as a result Shokoya-Eleshin Construction Ltd was invited as part of the UK Council's delegation to the Habitat II Conference on Urban Regeneration in June the same year.

Shokoya-Eleshin is seen (right) with Jack Straw, then Shadow Home Secretary, and Eric Armitage, Chief Executive of Northern British Housing Association, at the launch of a £1.5 million housing scheme in Blackburn, 1997.

The emblem of Shokoya-Eleshin Construction Ltd is a coat-of-arms representing Shokoya-Eleshin's ancestral descent from several royal houses in Nigeria. This photograph shows one of Shokoya-Eleshin's ancestors, the Alake of Abeokuta, taken by a royal court photographer in 1947.

Bill Morris, when Deputy General Secretary of the Transport and General Workers Union (TGWU), with Ron Todd (General Secretary). Born in Jamaica in 1938, Morris came to England in 1954 to join his widowed mother. After a baptism of fire in union posts at Hardy Spicers engineering firm in Birmingham, he became a full-time TGWU officer in 1973. His influence on national trade unionism emerged in 1979 when he was responsible for leading negotiations in the bus and coach industry as national Trade Group Secretary for Passenger Services. He was elected General Secretary of the TGWU in 1991. Morris has also served on a wide range of bodies including the European Community's Economic and Social Affairs Committee and the TUC's Race Relations Committee.

Gloria Mills worked as regional, national and then Equal Rights officer for the National Union of Public Employees (NUPE) before becoming the Director for Equal Opportunities at UNISON, Britain's biggest trade union, in 1993. In the following year she became the first Black woman to be elected to the TUC's ruling body, the General Council. She also sits on the Department of Employment and Education Race Relations and Employment Advisory Group and the TUC's Race Relations Committee. Through her campaigning work, Mills has fought for equal opportunities to be extended to women, Black people and lesbian and gay workers.

Albert O. Williamson-Taylor. He was born in 1959 in Bethnal Green to Nigerian parents. After studying building construction and structural engineering, he achieved chartered status in 1988, working for the engineers Pryce & Myers, and was involved in the early development of the quad bracket in aluminium alloy and planar glazing. As Senior Engineer and Associate for Anthony Hunt Associates, which he joined in 1988, he was responsible for several important designs, including the Sackler Galleries at the Royal Academy (1993) and the East India Dock floating footbridge (1995). In 1995 Williamson-Taylor became a founding partner in the practice of Adams Kara Taylor, a multicultural firm of consulting civil and structural engineers. Current projects include a millennium rainforest dome in Hanover, Germany, new library in Peckham with Alsop and Stormer, Loch Lomond footbridge in Scotland, London School of Economics Library with Sir Norman Foster & Partners, new cultural centre in Cardiff, Telecom tower in Malta, national gallery in Dublin and the design of the Black Cultural Archives in Brixton.

CHAPTER FIVE

CIVIC & POLITICAL

AFRICANS WHO BROUGHT DEMOCRACY TO LONDON

Londoners of African and Caribbean origin have contributed to the civic and political life of the capital in many ways. Being among its most oppressed citizens, these Black Londoners have been at the forefront of the struggles of the poor and disenfranchised. The brutality of slavery lit flames of political zeal, which inspired some of the finest political orators of the nineteenth century who helped to transform the campaign for the abolition of slavery into one of Britain's first mass political campaigns.

Among the first campaigners for democratic government and the freedom of the press, as leaders of the Chartist movement, were Robert Wedderburn who had docked in London from a British warship from Jamaica at the age of 17, and William Cuffay, one of the three London delegates to the Chartists' national convention, who was born in Chatham to a Jamaican ship's cook. Both were eventually deported for their seditious activities.

At the end of the Victorian age, another Black Londoner was to champion the poor and oppressed – John Archer. Although born in Liverpool to Barbadian and Irish parents, Archer settled in Battersea around 1890 and founded a photography studio in Battersea Park Road. John Archer has been credited with being the first British-born Black man to hold civic office in Britain, as councillor, alderman and mayor.

The ranks of often neglected women who have been political activists in London's history include Amy Ashwood Garvey. She co-founded the United Negro Improvement Association in collaboration with Marcus Aurelius Garvey (1914), which at its height in 1919 boasted a membership of 3 million people internationally. The Florence Mill Restaurant in London that she opened in 1929 with Sam Manning became a meeting place for Pan-Africanist intellectuals, writers, artists and visiting celebrities, and served as a centre of political discussion and organization for Black Londoners. Amy Ashwood

Garvey later became an active campaigner against the Fascist invasion of Ethiopia through the campaign group The International African Friends of Ethiopia.

POLITICAL ACTIVISM: THE BEST SOLUTION TO THE WORST INJUSTICE

What makes a man or woman enter political life? Undoubtedly, a certain amount of personal ambition. However, many were fired by the injustices that they had witnessed. To individuals such as Robert Wedderburn, who had witnessed his grandmother and his pregnant mother suffer under the slave-master's lash, the concept of freedom and justice was not an abstract ideal.

Privilege did not dampen John Archer's local commitment to the poor, the sick and the young in Battersea. Indeed, Archer believed that the greater one's economic capacity, the greater were his social and civic responsibilities.

Amy Ashwood Garvey's Pan-African ideals were fired not by the worst of human nature, but by witnessing its heights – the capacity of cultural survival. Through the role model of her grandmother, who retained memories of an Africa before her enslavement, Ashwood Garvey cultivated a cultural pride in her African heritage, which was rare for those who had undergone a British education. She was instrumental in the formation of political philosophies of Garveyism, Pan-Africanism and Black Power. In her striving to create support structures for the African Diaspora in London, Ashwood Garvey had an enormous impact on the political education of those were to lead the independent states of Africa and the Caribbean.

John Taylor, Lord Taylor of Warwick, became a life peer in 1996, succeeding the late Lord Pitt of Hampstead as the only Black person sitting in the House of Lords. A barrister since 1978, his involvement in community politics began as a Solihull borough councillor between 1986 and 1990. He participated in a Home Office/Department of Trade and Industry inner city think-tank in 1988 which led to his appointment as a special adviser to the Home Secretary and others. He came to national attention when he stood as prospective parliamentary candidate for Cheltenham in 1992 for the Conservative Party; despite his candidature receiving the support of the party hierarchy, racism within Cheltenham and among the local Conservatives manifested itself in a hostile campaign against Taylor's selection. His legal expertise and high profile have led to his involvement in the media and ground-breaking legal cases.

Mr. J. C. Archer, a photographer and a man of colour, who is the Progressive nominee for the Mayoralty of Battersea. A close fight is promised next Monday. "I am prepared," he has said, "to meet any man on a public platform on the question of colour prejudice." He has lived in Battersea twenty-three years.

John Archer, the first British-born Black man to hold civic office in Britain, as councillor, alderman and mayor. Archer was born in Liverpool in 1863 to a Barbadian father and an Irish mother. He settled in Battersea around 1890 with his Black Canadian wife, and opened a successful, award-winning photography studio in Battersea Park Road. A highly respected member of London's Black community, Archer was a friend of Samuel Coleridge-Taylor (*see* p. 23) and a delegate at the first Pan-Africanist Congress in Westminster town hall in 1900, when he was elected to the Executive Committee. Battersea was London's most progressive borough; when Archer was elected Mayor of Battersea in 1913, he declared, 'You have made history tonight . . . Battersea has done many things in its past, but the greatest thing that it has done is to show that it has no racial prejudice, and that it recognizes a man for the work he has done.' He played an active part in the civic life of the borough, especially in the spheres of tackling poverty and public health. He later became election agent for the Asian MP Shapurji Saklatvala, both as a Labour Party candidate and then as a Communist Party candidate. Archer died in 1932.

Amy Ashwood Garvey, political activist, impresario and historian. Born Amy Ashwood in Port Antonio, Jamaica, in 1897, she inherited a highly developed political sensibility from her grandmother, the daughter of Paramount Ruler of Juben (Ghana), in the independent state of the Ashanti Confederacy, who was brought to Jamaica as a slave. In 1914 she was co-founder, along with Marcus Aurelius Garvey (later to become her first husband), of the United Negro Improvement Association, which boasted a membership of 3 million people at its height in 1919. When she came to London in 1922 she quickly became aligned to the Pan-African movement, eventually chairing the fourth Pan-African Conference in 1945. In collaboration with Sam Manning, however, she is also credited with promoting the all-Negro revues that toured in London and Europe in the 1920s, with such critically acclaimed shows as *Hey, Hey!* and *Brown Sugar*. In 1929 Amy Ashwood and Sam Manning opened the Florence Mill Restaurant in London, which became a meeting-place for Pan-Africanist intellectuals, writers, artists and visiting celebrities.

When Fascist Italy invaded Abyssinia (Ethiopia) in 1935, Amy Ashwood Garvey became an active campaigner for the Abyssinians, founding the International African Friends of Abyssinia in 1936, and being one of the deputation that welcomed Haile Selassie when he arrived at Waterloo Station (*see* p. 83). During the Second World War, she negotiated with the Roosevelt government to offer wartime work to unemployed Jamaican women. This photograph depicts Amy Ashwood Garvey (right), wearing Ghana Kinte cloth robes, at 1 Basset Road, Ladbroke Grove, which she established as an African and Caribbean students' hostel and a women's resources centre in the 1950s. In later life she lived in Nigeria, Ghana and Liberia, studying the history and culture of these countries. She died in 1969.

Claudia Jones in the offices of the *West Indian Gazette*. Born in Trinidad in 1915, Jones emigrated to America when she was even. In 1956, however, she was deported from America because of her Communist links and she settled in London. She was a prominent Communist Party leader and trade unionist. On her arrival she formed a committee to support the victims of the McCarthyism that was sweeping America and driving so many left-wing activists and sympathizers to seek asylum in London. The following year, concerned that the Kenyan revolutionary movement was receiving biased treatment in the press, she initiated a bulletin comprising press cuttings and original articles. In 1958, the year of the Notting Hill riots, Claudia Jones founded the *West Indian Gazette*, the first ever mass-circulation Black newspaper in Britain. She continued to campaign on behalf of Kenyan political prisoners, and the issue of African independence and racial violence in Britain inspired her to form the African, Asian and Caribbean Organization. In 1958 Jones founded the Notting Hill Carnival to foster better relations between the Black and White community (*see* p. 124). She died in 1964.

Lord Pitt, with Lady Pitt, at his 80th birthday celebrations, 1993. David Thomas Pitt was born in St David's, Grenada, in 1913. He came to Britain to study medicine in 1932 after winning one of the island's top scholarships, qualifying in 1938 and eventually setting up his own general practice in Gower Street. His political life in London began in 1947 when he was part of a Commonwealth delegation of the Federation of the West Indies. Pitt played a full part in the political mobilization of postwar immigrants to Britain, as chairman of the Campaign Against Racial Discrimination, and as chairman of the Community Relations Commission from 1966 to 1977. He represented Hackney as a member of the London County Council and the Greater London Council in the 1960s. Although he was an unsuccessful parliamentary candidate for the seats of Hampstead and Clapham, he forged a path for the Black MPs who followed.

In 1985 he was created Baron Pitt of Hampstead, and the following year he became the first Black President of the British Medical Association. He was Patron of the Black Contractors Association until his death in 1994. This photograph shows him (right) at the inaugural gala dinner of the Parliamentary Black Caucus in 1987 (others shown are, from left to right, Keith Vaz, Bernie Grant, Ronald Delloms and Diane Abbott).

Bernie Grant, then Leader of Haringey Council, with Dolly Kiffin, head of the Broadwater Farm Youth Association, 1985. Born in Guyana in 1944, Dr Grant came to Britain in 1963. After working as a railway clerk and telephonist he became a full-time union official in 1978. He was elected as Labour councillor for Haringey in the same year, becoming leader in 1985. Grant came to prominence in the British press when he defended the young people whose frustration at police harassment resulted in the Broadwater Farm riot in which a police officer was killed. He went on to represent Tottenham as one of Britain's first Black MPs in 1987.

Gertrude Paul, who was appointed Commissioner for the Commission for Racial Equality (CRE) in 1980, and reappointed in 1984. The London-based CRE has been hugely instrumental in the fight for equality for all Black Britons. It has the powers to investigate cases of discrimination, to examine documents and to redress discriminatory practices. A total of fifteen Commissioners sit on the governing body; Mrs Paul was one of the earliest Black women to become a Commissioner.

Linda Bellos Adebowale. Born in London in 1950 and raised in Brixton, Bellos gained public recognition as part of the Greater London Council Women's Unit, and as Vice-Chair of her local Labour Party Black Section. She was elected leader of Lambeth Council in 1986. Her political philosophy has centred around two key issues: the involvement of working-class people in decision-making; and equal opportunities. Among the many initiatives while leading Lambeth Council she undertook was a move to increase the representation of Black contractors from two to one hundred. In the 1990s Bellos has forged a new career in broadcasting for Greater London Radio. She is also Co-ordinator of the Global Trade Centre in London, which exists to increase the trade links between the Black community in the UK and internationally.

Merle Amory, the first Afro-Caribbean woman to lead a district council in Britain. Born in 1958 on the West Indian island of St Kitts, Amory came to Britain at the age of five, settling in London, and joined the Labour Party in 1974. She stood as councillor for the Stonebridge ward at the age of twenty-three, and later for Queen's Park. She became leader of Brent Council in 1986, the first Black woman council leader in Brent and the youngest Labour council leader in London. As leader of the London Transport Board for the GLC in 1987–8 she was responsible for the regulation of all transport in London.

Diane Abbott, with Bernie Grant. Born in 1953, Abbott was educated at Cambridge University before working for the Home Office. She has also been a member of Westminster City Council (1982–6) and a reporter for TV-AM. In 1987 she was elected Labour MP for Stoke Newington, becoming a member of the Labour Party's National Executive in 1991.

Paul Boateng in front of the Palace of Westminster. Born in Hackney in 1952 of Ghanaian–English origin, Boateng took an active interest in politics from an early age, joining the Labour Party at the age of fifteen. His skills in political rhetoric were honed by his training as a solicitor in the 1970s, and later as a barrister. Boateng represented Walthamstow on the Greater London Council before becoming MP for Brent South in 1987. An active member of the Opposition for a decade, he is now the most senior-ranking Black politician in the House of Commons, becoming Under-Secretary of State for Health in the Labour government of 1997. Boateng is also a Methodist lay preacher and former Vice-Moderator of the World Council of Churches Programme to Combat Racism. In 1988 he won the prestigious Martin Luther King Memorial Prize for social and racial justice.

Ambrosine Neil. A tireless community and race relations campaigner, Ambrosine Neil came to Brixton in 1962 to pursue a career in dress design. She was founder member of the Parents Association for Educational Advance in 1976, and was elected Labour councillor for Brent in 1982, although she gained notoriety by 'crossing the floor' of the council chamber to join the Conservatives, thus turning Brent into a hung council after twelve years under Labour. Brent later passed into Conservative control, but Neil lost her seat in 1986 when she stood as Conservative councillor for Manor Ward, Brent South.

Rudolph Daley trying out an exercise bike while opening Lambeth's fourth day centre for people with severe learning difficulties, late 1980s. Daley came to Britain in 1958 from Jamaica. After a career in administration he was elected to Lambeth Council in 1986, becoming Mayor of Lambeth in 1988.

Valda Louise James as Mayor of Islington, 1988. James was
born in 1927. She came to Britain in 1961 and raised her
six children alone in conditions of some hardship while
working in catering, dressmaking and nursing. In 1986 she
became the first Black woman to be elected to Islington
Council, where she applied her experience of raising a
family in difficult circumstances to her work on the Social
Services Committee. Two years later she transformed the
face of Islington local government by becoming mayor,
with her daughter as Deputy Mayor.

Randolph Beresford with his wife, displaying his MBE outside the gates of Buckingham Palace, 1986. Born
in Guyana in 1914, Beresford was already a skilled carpenter and contractor before he came to London in
1953. He became an active member of the Amalgamated Society of Woodworkers, sitting on the London
Federation of Trades Councils in 1962. A councillor for eighteen years for White City Ward, he became
Mayor of Hammersmith and Fulham in 1975. His contribution to the local community was recognized
when he received the British Empire Medal in 1979 and was made an MBE in 1986. Since retiring in
1979, Randolph Beresford has helped to establish in Ghana two sister clubs to the Mission Dine Club,
Willesden, a luncheon club for West Indian seniors.

CHAPTER SIX

LONDON INTERNATIONAL

Nationality and our sense of place are often constrained by the notion of a world in which populations remain within a single geographical region, and the notion of one's national loyalty is fixed and simple. 'Black Londoners', we shall see, have been part of a shifting population, in which movement has occurred to and from Africa and the West Indies, not just among individuals, but among different generations of the same family.

Throughout this book an attempt has been made to broaden the concept of what it is to be a 'Londoner' in order to include those who themselves may not immediately perceive themselves as such. It may be contended that instead of sticking rigidly to birth or length of residence, it may be more useful to assess Black Londoners' 'credentials', by more complex notions, such as contribution, sense of belonging, impact upon a wider community, and international consciousness.

One group which has often been forgotten in our focus on Africa's disempowerment at the turn of the century has been that of African kings and queens, and their emissaries. It is important, however, that the movement of African royal houses and diplomatic corps be acknowledged, since their activities became particularly intensive in the run up to the 'scramble for Africa' by Europe. If we do not acknowledge them, we risk the confirming the stereotype of Africa as a helpless child. It must be remembered that before military annexation of African territory, many African leaders had instigated protracted diplomatic missions to London. They would arrive via Greenwich, and then make their way up the Thames to Westminster.

Such a journey was made by Chief of Bamangwato, of the British protectorate of Bechuanaland, now known as Botswana. Chief Khama led a deputation to London, which included Chief Sebele of the Bakwena and Chief Bathoen of the Bangwaketse, in 1895 to see Queen Victoria. Their diplomatic mission aimed to prevent their territory from being transferred to Cecil Rhodes's British company in South Africa. The deputation was a success, and Bechuanaland became a protectorate, against the encroachment of White settlers. This deputation was to leave an indelible mark on the memories of Londoners. These great African chiefs' dignified carriage, flamboyant dress and Christian piety, combined with the moral appeal of their cause, made them welcomed visitors. Several years later when the grandson of chief Khama entered London newspapers for quite different reasons, the memory of his forebears was invoked.

As in all walks of life, the diplomatic arena has seen significant changes in the role of women. Women's disposition for bonding and establishing trust in new environments and their conciliatory style has perhaps made them natural diplomats. The late twentieth century has seen this natural advantage put to international use, with increased representation among the senior members of an international diplomatic corps. Mrs Agnes Aggrey-Orleans came to London in the 1960s as Education Counsellor at the Ghanaian Embassy; today she is the High Commissioner in Geneva, a highly influential posting.

Interestingly enough, the Aggrey-Orleans have another High Commissioner among their ranks: Mrs Agnes Aggrey-Orleans' husband – who was appointed High Commissioner to the Ghana Embassy in London in 1998. Thus, the Aggrey-Orleans, like many others, have had ongoing London connections, which are used by the embassies of Africa and the Caribbean to make their national voices heard effectively among their international peers.

When one's children have been raised and educated in London and one's everyday existence is living and working in the capital, who can say that one is not a Black Londoner at the end of the diplomatic mission when it is time to be called 'home'?

Dr Kwame Nkrumah (second right) at the Commonwealth Conference of Prime Ministers, London, 1960. Born in the Gold Coast (now Ghana) in 1909, Nkrumah became an active member of the Pan-Africanist movement in London, which worked for political independence from imperial domination, in the 1940s and 1950s. He was also editor of the *New African* in 1945–7. He went on to become Prime Minister of the Gold Coast in 1952, then Prime Minister of the independent Ghana in 1957, the first independent African state of the modern age. Although a product of Western education, Kwame Nkrumah made a point of wearing robes of Kente cloth as a statement of national identity and pride. He died in 1972.

Eleazar Chukwuemeka (Emeka) Anyaoku. Born in 1933, Eleazar Anyaoku became Executive Assistant in the Commonwealth Development Corporation, in London and Lagos, in 1959, and a member of the Nigerian delegation to the United Nations in 1962. For three decades he acted as Commonwealth Observer of elections, referenda and talks, one of the most senior positions in international diplomacy, and was based in London. Since 1990, Anyaoku has been Secretary-General to the Commonwealth, based at Marlborough House in London.

Mabel Dove at the counting of the votes for the seat of Ga in Ghana in the 1950s, as the first woman to become a member of the Legislative Assembly of Ghana. Before her political career, Mabel Dove was a prominent West African journalist in London.

Nnamdi Azikiwe, journalist turned statesman. Born in 1904, he was Editor-in-Chief of the *African Morning Post*, Accra, from 1934 to 1937, and then of the *West African Pilot* until 1945. From 1945 Azikiwe was a representative of the National Council for Nigeria and the Cameroons, which began as a London student movement. He questioned Britain's continued domination of her subject nations and took the British government to task on democracy and human rights. In 1963 he became the first President of Nigeria, having been Governor-General and Commander-in-Chief from 1960. He was Joint President of the Anti-Slavery Society, based in London, in 1970, and wrote extensively on economics, politics, history and poetry. Azikiwe died in 1995.

Mrs Azikiwe, born Flora Ogbenyeanu Ogoegbunamn, awarding a plaque to A.E. Hoffman, Chairman of the Palm Shipping Co., 1961.

Sir Edward Asafu Adjaye, the first High Commissioner for Ghana (1958). Having graduated in Philosophy and Law at University College London in 1925, he won the Profumo Prize in law in 1927 and went on to enjoy a distinguished legal and political career, playing an active part in Ghana's transition to independence. He was the kind of intellectual heavyweight needed to grapple with the new trade contracts with Britain that were forged after independence was granted in 1957.

Sir Edward Asafu Adjaye signing the UK–Ghana Air Services Agreement in 1958. He was knighted in 1960 and made a fellow of University College London the following year.

H.V.H. Sekyi, High Commissioner to Ghana, en route to present his Letters of Commission to the Queen, 1970s.

Sir Seretse Khama arriving for talks at the Commonwealth Relations Office, Whitehall, 1950. Born in 1925, Khama was the son of an African chief of the Bamangwato, a British protectorate of Bechuanaland. He came to London to study law, but was exiled by the British state when he married a White woman, Ruth Williams, a *cause célébre* that enlivened dreary postwar London. Because of this he was only allowed to return to Britain in 1956 on renouncing his chieftainship, and it is now clear that Britain succumbed to pressure from the South African government, then pursuing a policy of racial separation, to deny Khama his rights. South Africa held the key to Britain's status as a world power because of her uranium reserves, which were vital for Britain's nuclear programme. In 1966 Khama became the first Prime Minister of an independent Botswana, and was knighted.

The dictator Dr Hastings Banda on a state visit to London in the 1960s. Hastings Banda was a GP in London from 1945 to 1953 and represented Nyasaland at the Pan-African Congress of 1945. He was President of Malawi from 1966 to 1994. Below, Mrs Banda and the Duke of Edinburgh.

Haile Selassie on a state visit to London, October 1954. When Abyssinia was invaded by Italy in 1935 the violent and duplicitous nature of imperialism was exposed anew. Black Londoners, through such organizations as the International African Friends of Abyssinia, united with mass movements in Africa and the West Indies to formulate a new ideology of colonial liberation.

Send-off party given by Mrs Kwesie Armah for the outgoing wives of councillors at the Ghana High Commission, 1965. Women at the High Commission often acted as administrators and were responsible for establishing and maintaining links between Ghana and London's Black and indigenous communities, as well as between national and international embassies.

George and Dorothy Owanabae with their son, Anthony, 1964. Originally from Owarri, Nigeria, Mr and Mrs Owanabae lived for three years in Wales, where Mr Owanabae was a student, before settling in Kilburn, north-west London, in 1964. In the same year, Mr Owanabae qualified as an accountant. Mrs Owanabae later became a fashion and beauty consultant and fashion designer, starting her own company. The Owanabaes returned to Nigeria in the early 1980s.

Mrs Asafu Adjaye welcoming M. de Guiringaud to the Ghana High Commission in France. Formerly Martha Violet Randolph, Mrs Asafu Adjaye was one of the many 'first ladies' of the independent African High Commissions to help to build trust and good relations within the world of international diplomacy in the post-colonial era. In addition to being Ghana's first High Commissioner to the UK (*see* pp. 79–80), Sir Edward Asafu Adjaye was Ghana's first Ambassador to France (1957–61).

John (twelve) and William (eleven), the sons of the President of Liberia, discovering how a TV set works, at the Radio Show, Earls Court, 1957. They are accompanied by their tutor, Mr P. Fry.

Winnie Mandela (centre) with members of the Commonwealth Secretariat, 1986. The Commonwealth Secretariat, based in Pall Mall, London, has been the administrative centre of the Commonwealth since 1965. The fifty-four independent nations and former British colonies that make up the Commonwealth have campaigned for human rights and humanitarian causes for over three decades, epitomized by the campaign against apartheid in South Africa. Under the Harare Declaration of 1991 the Commonwealth committed itself to the encouragement of democracy and good government, which has led to a reduction in the number of military and one-party states among its members, although the execution of the writer and environmental campaigner Ken Saro-Wiwa by the military government of Nigeria in 1995 led to the immediate suspension of that country's membership. The emphasis in the Commonwealth is now increasingly towards trade, investment and the global economy.

CHAPTER SEVEN

CHURCH LEADERS

As early as 1765, Africans and West Indians came to London to be ordained as priests in the Church of England. As their numbers and seniority increased, they came to be consecrated as bishops. Examples are the Rt Revd J.T. Holly, who was consecrated Bishop of Haiti in 1874; the Rt Revd Samuel D. Ferguson, Bishop of Cape Palmas (now Liberia) in 1885; and the Rt Revd Isaac Oluwole, Assistant Bishop of Lagos in 1893. The pilgrimage of Black bishops from all over the globe to Westminster Abbey and St Paul's Cathedral may challenge some of our preconceptions of the involvement of Black people in the Anglican Church.

One particularly influential minister who forces us to reassess the involvement of Black Londoners in organized religion is Dr Harold Moody, Congregationalist minister and one-time head of the London Missionary Society. Such figures as Moody and the Trinidadian temperance lecturer Henry Sylvester Williams demand that we reappraise the concept of the missionary as being both White and Africa-bound. These ministers had a considerable presence in London and an enormous popular following among all ethnic groups.

THE MODERN BISHOPS OF THE INNER-CITY

The Rt Revd Wilfred Wood, Bishop of Croydon, represents the experiences of postwar mass immigration. Originally from Barbados, his settlement in London forced Bishop Wood to be aware of the harshness of life for new immigrants, and the problems of the inner city. As a strong advocate of a relevant church, he became one of the founder members of Paddington Churches Housing Association, thus encouraging the dramatic growth of housing associations in general and, in particular, Black housing associations.

Despite the long association of London's African-Caribbean communities with the

Anglican Church, they have only recently had the opportunity to make their presence felt in the decision-making body of the church – the General Synod. Between 1990 and 1996, for example, the Rt Revd Dr John Sentamu served on the General Synod, while maintaining his early links with the prison service as a committee member of the National Council for the Care and Resettlement of Offenders, the Family Welfare Association and the Health Advisory Committee of Her Majesty's Prisons. Now the Bishop of Stepney, he has defined his mission as 'To seek God's rule of justice, righteousness, peace and love; to be part of God's movement of change, to reach out with God's love to human need, and to be a vision-bearer for the area.'

Isaac P. Dickerson (standing centre), evangelical minister and temperance lecturer. Dickerson was born a slave in Virginia in 1852. When he was emancipated he became a teacher at a missionary school in Chattanooga and travelled to Britain with the Jubilee Singers, a choir that toured America and Europe to raise funds for Fisk University for Negro education. Dickerson remained in Britain when the choir returned to the USA in 1872 and studied to become a minister at Edinburgh University. He toured as an evangelist throughout Europe and Palestine, and when he began a small mission of his own in Plumstead, he supported himself by lecturing on these regions throughout Britain. Dickerson was a cheerful and well-liked figure in his local community.

George Makippe, known as Watto or Watteau. Makippe was born a slave in equatorial Africa and was freed and converted to Christianity by David Livingstone. He came to Britain as a young man in 1886 as one of the bearers of Dr Livingstone's coffin at his state funeral. Makippe was appointed gardener to James E. Vanner, in Chislehurst, where he worked for thirty years, being remembered by his employer in his will. He then worked as gardener for a Mr Williamson for another twenty years. He was a local celebrity both in Chislehurst and in London, and his picture was taken by many court photographers. Makippe was an active member of the Wesleyan church and a celebrated organ-blower for many years. He married an Englishwoman, who bore him three sons, and he died at a great age in 1931.

Wilfred Wood. Born in Barbados in 1936, Wood came to London in 1962 and served as curate, then honorary curate, of St Thomas with St Stephen, Shepherd's Bush, until 1974. Being struck by the harsh conditions that Black immigrants had to undergo and by the problems of the inner city, Wood maintained an active interest in race relations and social justice in London. He was a founder member of the Paddington Churches Housing Association, as well as of Berbice Housing Co-operative, Notting Hill Community Association and the Carib Housing Association for Black Elders. He was appointed the Bishop of London's Race Relations Officer in 1966 and Chairman of the Institute of Race Relations in 1971. He has been Bishop of Croydon since 1985.

Paul Keynes Douglas, Jamaican orator, reciting a reading from 'Pa Pa God' on Caribbean Sunday at a London church.

The Rt Revd Dr John Sentamu outside the church that he helped to restore in Tulse Hill, 1988. Sentamu was born in 1949 in Uganda where he enjoyed an illustrious career as Chief Magistrate and Judge of the High Court before he was forced to leave the country in the 1970s because of his criticism of Idi Amin's violations of human rights. After studying theology at Cambridge University, he became a minister in the Church of England, holding positions in Cambridge and London before serving as vicar of Tulse Hill from 1983 to 1990. He was a member of the General Synod of the Church of England until 1996, when he was appointed Bishop of Stepney. Much of Dr Sentamu's work has been concerned with the welfare of prisoners and the ethnic minorities.

Garth Moody (crouching, right) with his family, on holiday in Jamaica, 1940s. Born in London in 1925, the younges
child of Dr Harold Moody (*see* p. 47), Garth Moody trained as a pilot in 1944, although the war finished before h
training was completed. He then spent ten years in the Civil Service in London before emigrating to New Zealand i
1958, where he ran a hostel for Maori teenagers. Returning to London, he followed in his father's footsteps by becomin
a Congregationalist minister in Wimbledon in 1971, combining Christian ministry with a strong social commitment. I
1985 he continued his ministry in Nottinghamshire.

CHAPTER EIGHT

TRANSPORT

From the turn of the century employment within the British Merchant Navy brought many Black Londoners to the capital – men such as Joseph Adolphus Bruce at the turn of the century, and Orlando Martins and Earl Cameron during the First and Second World Wars. Black Londoners have maintained strong links with London's transport industries throughout the twentieth century. In the 1940s there was an influx of Black British war-workers from the West Indies, charged with the responsibilities of keeping road and rail transport moving as part of the war effort. Many Black Londoners benefited from the strong connections of the military with the transport industries, through companies such as Alliance Haulage, Lambeth. It was a regimental link that gave Hector Watson his first job after the war – he went on to establish one of the first Black-owned haulage transport companies in Britain.

Many West Indians were recruited to work in London through the Barbados Migrants Liaison Service (BMLS) (1948–56), a body created by the government of Barbados and encouraged by the British government to tackle unemployment in both countries and labour shortages, originally for London Transport. It organized recruitment campaigns, medicals, training programmes for applicants, examinations, transportation and settlement loans. The BMLS proved such an efficient model that it was adopted by the British government to encourage and settle new immigrants to Britain, not simply for London Transport but for the National Health Service, British Rail and the hotel and catering industries. In 1956 the organization was renamed the Migrants Liaison Service and extended to cover other West Indian islands.

Although proportionately small in numbers, Black transport workers in London were highly visible in their employment, and became an integral feature of the life of the capital. Their ubiquity has made London into one of the most cosmopolitan cities in the world.

For many workers, difficult conditions were made worse by the prejudiced attitudes of co-workers and superiors alike. 'Blacks were never given senior positions, regardless of clear ability or years of service. You could be a foreman but never a station master', according to Mr Ben Davis who has worked for London Transport for forty-seven years. 'Things have only recently changed.' While some had to fight their battles alone, others benefited from the increasing political assertion of a Black community growing in size and confidence. One important example of this was the West Indian Standing Conference's 1967 campaign against the *de facto* 'colour bar' against Black inspectors.

Joe Clough was one of London's first Black bus drivers. In 1908 he was the driver of the no. 11 on the route fro Liverpool Street to Wormwood Scrubs. He worked for the London General Bus Company which later became known London Transport. Mr Clough originally came to London from Jamaica in 1906. He married the daughter of a ci publican. Mr Clough went on to deploy the driving skills he had honed on the streets of London, working as a ambulan driver in France during the First World War. After 1918, Mr Clough left the city and settled in Bedford, working for local bus company and then went on to run his own taxi firm.

B. Johnston and J. Joff at their tea break, 1942. This photograph of two Black workers, one from Jamaica and the other from the Gambia, reminds us of the wartime service provided to London Transport by Black people. Many Black people served as drivers, agricultural workers, engineers, coal miners and munitions workers as well as in the armed forces. Mr Johnston had already served in the Navy before 1942, having had a lucky escape when his ship was torpedoed; before that he was reputedly a chauffeur for Mae West.

Ben Davis (back row, left) with the Emergency Breakdown crew, Neasden, 1959. In 1997 Davis celebrated forty-seven years of service for London Transport. Born in 1932, he began work as an engineer at Ealing Common in 1951, joining the Breakdown Emergency Service in 1959. Despite much initial opposition to the presence of a Black engineer in this all-White service, Davis persevered and was one of the crew that drove a lorry to Moorgate in 1982 to aid the survivors of the train disaster there.

Cynthia Palmer (left) clearing snow from Leytonstone Underground station in the harsh winter of 1963. Cynthia Palmer has now retired, but still conducts customer surveys for London Transport.

Ken Harper, bus driver, with his children, 1960s. Although London Transport helped to sustain many Black families in postwar Britain, there was little equality of employment. Despite the mass recruitment of Black workers in the 1960s, not a single Black bus inspector had been appointed by 1967, the year of *The Unsquare Deal: London's Black Colour Bar*, an influential report by the West Indian Standing Conference. This report revealed the restrictive employment practices and the racism of most White garage managers and made several recommendations to remedy the situation. These recommendations are now an accepted feature of employment practice.

Mrs A. Hart, bus conductor at Stockwell Garage, 1962, a classic image currently on show at the London Transport Museum. What this image does not show are the hardships, indignities and heroism of these women who managed to survive in jobs which were still male dominated and to endure the hostile elements of the London streets. Black women bus conductors triumphed over these adversities, winning the respect of their peers, and providing models of employment for a new generation of Black British women.

Joyce Edwards, railwaywoman on the London Underground for thirty-three years. Edwards came to Britain from Barbados in 1958 to study nursing at Leavesden Hospital, Watford. In 1960, however, she changed career, becoming a London Transport railwaywoman. After eight years as a ticket collector at Marble Arch and four as a relief ticket collector, she moved to Wembley Park station and spent twenty years there – the most rewarding of her career, she says. In 1993 she received a special certificate of service marking her thirty-three years' work for London Underground.

Many women were employed by London Transport in catering on an industrial scale, as large-scale demand took home-grown catering skills well beyond the domestic sphere. Black women met the challenge of creative menus within prescribed budgets. Mrs Norma Medford, of Stockwell Garage, won the Hotelolympia International Hotel and Catering Exhibition challenge cup and gold medal for the industrial catering section in 1966. The silver medallist, Miss Anita Smith of Acton Works, was also Black. Marva Braham, another award-winner, had one of her recipes immortalized in the London Transport Museum as 'Mrs B's Recipe for Caribbean Fish'. Such women introduced diversity to their menus and a richness to traditional English fare that reflected their cultural origins. Miss Lafinmakin (right) serving tea in a London Transport canteen, 1965.

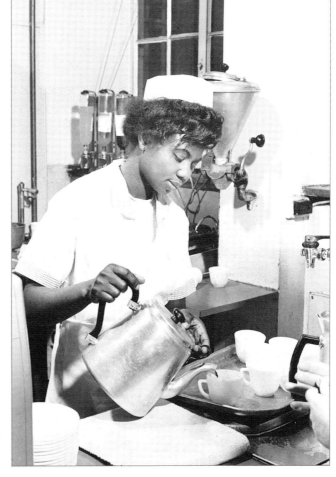

Centralized canteens were a necessity in an industry characterized by shift work and unsocial hours. British employers such as London Transport often recruited Black women directly from the West Indies to fill both traditional and non-traditional job vacancies, giving them extensive training. This photograph shows Mrs Merna Miller being crowned London Transport Catering Queen for 1971. This competition was designed to add glamour and excitement to a job which was as much physically demanding and a test of endurance as it was skilled.

A Black woman bus inspector in the 1970s. The first line of promotion for the ordinary busman and bus woman was inspector – from acting inspector to silver badge inspector and then gold badge inspector. Inspectors commanded a better salary and conditions of work, as well as higher status. It took many years, however, for the 'colour bar' to cease operating so that Black bus workers could become inspectors alongside their White colleagues.

The shared experiences of the Underground are part of what it is to be a 'Londoner'. There are unwritten codes of behaviour – silence, strict observation of personal space, avoidance of eye contact. Many recall when they first learnt 'the rules' of the London Underground, and compare these with some amusement to public behaviour in Africa and the West Indies.

CHAPTER NINE

Educationalists, Writers & Scientists

Black Londoners have sought access to learning as a means of emancipation from the constraints of Empire, class, race and geographical location. While some came to London on scholarships from Africa and the West Indies sponsored by Church missionary societies or wealthy parents, others came as travellers or workers. In their plans for the future, education and training featured significantly.

Students and educationalists of African, Caribbean and Asian origin were among the first to raise the clarion call against racial oppression within the British Empire. Individuals such as Trinidadian law student and temperance lecturer Henry Sylvester Williams had the opportunity to observe at first hand the conditions of life in the West Indies, and racism on the streets of London, and make the link between racial oppression and the political reality of Empire. It was Williams who issued a call in 1898 for a world conference on Black people to take place in 1900.

Before the mass recruitment in the transport industry and the health service, students were the most numerically significant group of the Black population, and were key allies of the resident Black population. Both groups relied upon each other for political organization and self-defence, in the broadest sense. The gathering of different national and ethnic groups, all of whom were under imperial control, resulted in better mutual understanding and provided a new perspective on the Empire, a perspective that was at odds with imperial propaganda. Personal contact meant that different ethnic groups could reject the stereotypes inherited about each other, which made possible the political mobilization of the myriad independence movements of Africa and the West Indies. Thus to study in London became an education in Pan-Africanism.

Despite the influx of students from Africa and the West Indies to London, few were accepted in the professional life of London after graduation. While many had always intended to return to Africa and the West Indies, it also became clear that to remain in London to practise professionally was not always an option. Dr Harold Moody, for example, was refused employment at King's College Hospital despite being among the highest achievers in his year as a medical student in the same hospital. This stimulated his ambition to open his four London surgeries. Likewise the father of the famous London composer, Samuel Coleridge-Taylor, had to return to Ghana in order to practise as a surgeon, where he was later to become Surgeon-General.

Patterns of professional discrimination continued in the 1950s. Like many who came to London to study, Beryl Gilroy was among the West Indies educational élite. Yet before being allowed to teach, she was forced to work as a washer-up at Joe Lyons' restaurant chain, in a factory and as a lady's maid. Her titanic battle for professional recognition led to her appointment as one of the first Black headmistresses within a mainstream London school.

A milestone in changing the educational climate occurred in 1966 when New Beacon Books was founded by John La Rose. Since then, he has been responsible for the publication and dissemination of books by Black writers such as Sam Sevlon, Derek Walcott and C.L.R. James. These publications have not only impacted upon the Black communities in the UK, but have altered the paradigms of the British educational establishment. Without such books, multiculturalist approaches to education would not have been possible.

Other individuals such as Gloria Lock have played a major part in introducing the books of African-Caribbean writers into mainstream education and the public at large. By offering teaching advice and support, and assistance to students working on class projects, Gloria Lock's remit as specialist Afro-Caribbean Librarian for some twelve libraries in Wandsworth includes stock acquisition, display, training, publication, liaising with the public and educationalists, and organizing events. The result is a welcoming and supportive environment for all seekers of knowledge on a multicultural community.

Mary Lucinda Rice. Born in Plumstead in 1882, the daughter of Dr George Rice (*see* p. 44–5), Mary Rice lived in the family home in Sutton from 1919. It was from this house, called Sagamore, that she ran the Sagamore Preparatory School from 1938. The family archive that she maintained on the Rice family was rescued from the local council rubbish dump by a Black council worker, Mr W. Ryder of Croydon. Her mother's family, the Cooks, owned Borstall Farm and were a wealthy family of contractors who played an active part in civic life.

Students in the 1940s. Many people of Afro-Caribbean descent came to London as students. Some became permanent residents, others returned home, and a third group came and went, forming part of London's shifting population. Colonial secondary education was modelled closely on the English school system and largely administered by English men and women who set exams from the English examination boards. In theory a student could transfer from a classroom in Jamaica to a classroom in England without having to make any adjustment. Ironically, while British schools have moved away from more traditional teaching methods, some West Indian islands have retained them, with the result that Barbados, among other countries, has a higher literacy rate than England itself. Many Black teachers who were educated in Britain returned to Africa and the West Indies equipped to challenge the Europe-focused education systems of their countries. They include Dr Francis Akanu Ibiam, Principal of the Hope Waddell Training Institute, in Calabar, Nigeria, who went on to become Governor of the Eastern Region after independence.

Recruitment panel at Nigeria House, London, for the new University of Nigeria, at Nsukka, 1960 (Dr Nnamdi Azikiwe, chairman, is second left). From the 1950s, with the prospect of independence, came the need to reform the institutions of higher learning in Africa and the West Indies. Although ancient Africa boasted some of the earliest universities in the history of civilization, under colonialism the education of the élite was in the hands of their colonial masters; in Nigeria, for example, only 10 per cent of all civil service posts were held by Africans in 1945. New universities and colleges had to be built to educate Africans and West Indians so that they could take up key posts in their own countries, and Black graduates were recruited in abundance from London and elsewhere.

Gloria Lock (née Johnson) with her mother just before travelling to London from Sierra Leone in 1960. She studied at the University of London and Royal Holloway College, then taught English and librarianship in Sierra Leonean, Nigerian and British colleges and universities. Since 1985 she has been specialist Afro-Caribbean Librarian in Wandsworth, with responsibilities for twelve branch libraries. Lock has made Wandsworth the model for the dissemination of information on Black people, both locally and internationally, through several landmark exhibitions, such as *Focus on Africa* (1987) and *1492 and All That* (1992). She has also produced a series of postcards on local Black historical figures which challenge prevailing historical assumptions. In 1992 she won the Holt Jackson Library Association Award for Community Initiative and Good Practice.

The grandsons of Haile Selassie, the former Emperor of Ethiopia, when students at the University of London, 1950s. Since the earliest contact with Europeans, African chiefs had sent their children to be educated in London. Western education then became a tool of imperial control, but eventually provided the seeds of the Empire's destruction, as it was the London-based Black students who became the fiercest campaigners against British imperialism and leaders of the first independent nation states of Africa and the West Indies. Nigerian students formed the largest Afro-Caribbean political grouping at King's College, London, and founded one of the most powerful independence movements of the 1940s, the National Council for Nigeria and the Cameroons, renamed the National Council for Nigerian Citizens in 1944. The organization had an ideology of Pan-Africanism, such that its first president, Herbert Macaulay, was a West Indian nationalist. Nnandi Azikiwe rose from the ranks of the NCNC to become the first leader of independent Nigeria in 1963.

Charles Ifejika who received the Lee Valley Business Innovation Award in 1996. Born in Nigeria in 1957, Ifejika came to London at the age of three and trained as an engineer. After receiving hospital treatment in 1986 for an eye infection caused by the build up of harmful chemicals behind his contact lenses, he embarked upon his own research into more effective methods of eliminating bacteria from contact lenses, inventing a means of using electrical charges to do so. The Ifejika contact lens cleaning device has attracted the support of many academic, medical and research bodies. As a result he has obtained funding to conduct clinical trials so that the design can be exploited commercially.

John La Rose, political and cultural activist. Born in 1927, La Rose came to London from Trinidad, where he had made a significant impact on political life as General Secretary of the West Indian Independence Party and in the trade union movement. From his North London base he founded the Caribbean Artists' Movement (1966), the Caribbean Education and Community Workers' Association (1969) and the Black Parents' Movement (1975). He is also one of Britain's leading Black publishing pioneers as publisher of New Beacon Books since 1966 and founder of the International Book Fair of Radical Black and Third World Books. The publication and dissemination of books by such Black writers as Sam Selvon, Derek Walcott and C.L.R. James has made the multicultural approach to education possible. La Rose is also a poet and essayist in his own right.

Jessica and Eric Huntley, co-founders of Bogle L'Ouverture Publications in 1969. Among the earliest Black independent publishers in Britain, they are also founders and co-directors of the International Book Fair of Radical Black and Third World Books. Jessica Huntley also plays a leading role as an educator, not only in the Supplementary School movement responding to the crisis in the response of the educational system to Black children, but also by providing educational and equal opportunities consultancy.

Andrew Salkey, writer, editor and teacher. Born in Panama in 1928 to Jamaican parents, Salkey travelled widely, coming to London in 1952 to study at London University. He spent the next twenty-four years in the capital as freelance broadcaster, book reviewer, teacher, narrator and writer, contributing to a host of political and literary journals and writing books across the fields of non-fiction, novels, poetry and children's stories. He has also written some fifty plays and other features, mostly for radio. His work deals with the themes of boundaries between people and national territories and the impact when these boundaries are crossed. These themes are as present in the folk tales of the Caribbean that he has retold, especially about the Anancy character, as in political studies of race and colonialism. Salkey was Professor of Writing at Hampshire College, Massachusetts from 1976 to his death in 1995.

Ben Okri, writer and journalist. Okri was born in Nigeria in 1959 and came to London at the age of four. His writing career began even before he had finished studying comparative literature at the University of Essex, with the publication of *Flowers and Shadows* in 1980. This was followed by *The Landscape Within* (1982). In 1987 he was shortlisted for the Commonwealth Prize, and the following year for the Guardian Fiction Prize, for *Incidents at the Shrine* and *Stars of the Curfew*. He won the Booker Prize in 1994 for *The Famished Road*. Okri has contributed to several leading newspapers and journals, including the *Guardian*, the *Observer* and the *New Statesman*. He now lives in north-west London.

CHAPTER TEN

NEWS & NEWSMAKERS

The individuals, events and institutions which have had an impact upon the cultural and political life of Black London are too numerous to mention. However, this chapter attempts to record some of the factors that have been the most important influences.

Black Londoners of African, Caribbean and Asian origin were among the first to raise the clarion call against racial oppression at the First Pan-African Conference on 23–25 July 1900 at Westminster Town Hall. This conference attempted to take steps to influence public opinion on existing proceedings and conditions affecting the 'Natives' in the various parts of the Empire, in particular, South Africa, West Africa and the British West Indies. It was at this conference that Dr W.E.B. DuBois, the Black American scholar and leader, declared that 'the problem of the twentieth century is the problem of the colour line'.

Significantly, John Archer, the first Black mayor of a London borough, Samuel Coleridge-Taylor, London-born musician and composer of Ghanaian origin, and Trinidadian law student and temperance lecturer Henry Sylvester Williams helped to organize the conference. One of its sponsors included the Asian ex-MP Dadabhai Naoroji. Here we have an early example of African-Caribbean and Asian Londoners' political solidarity. (John Archer later became election agent for his political mentor Saklavatla, one of the first Asian MPs.)

The organized political responses of the Black community have often come from events which have been far from organized but rather random and symptomatic of deeper social issues – the killing of a Black woman during an illegal police raid, the unexplained death in police custody of a young man, and so on. Such were the shooting of Cherry Groce, the killing of Cynthia Jarrett and the death of Colin Roach – events which affected Black Londoners but which attracted the protest of Londoners of all races, events which brought home to the Black community the fact that change could be brought about by both organized and disorganized mass protest and by mobilization through the political processes. Either way, apathy was simply not an option.

The cultural impact of Black Londoners on London life has been significant, from youth sub-culture and music, to fashion, food and literature. The Africa Centre and the Notting Hill Carnival are symbols of the contribution that Black Londoners have made to one of the most cosmopolitan cities in the world.

Alex Pascal (left) interviewing for the radio programme *Black Londoners*. Pascal came to London from Grenada in 1959 where he had founded the island's first folk group and he soon built up a reputation as an experienced compere at some of the capital's leading nightclubs. In 1969 he formed the Alex Pascal Singers, which drew upon both African and Caribbean traditions of performance. In 1974 he was invited to host *Black Londoners* on Radio London. One of the longest-running radio programmes hosted by a Black presenter, it was unique in its mix of music and community news and interviews. Pascal was an early champion of Soca Calypso and African music, and a pioneer in the development of Afro-Caribbean teaching resources for schools. He also acted as educational adviser for several television companies, and wrote and recorded stories and music for radio and television. He is a highly respected member of the Black community in London, chairing the Notting Hill Carnival in 1986.

Trevor McDonald. Born in 1939, McDonald came to London in 1962 as a reporter for Radio Trinidad, covering the Independence Conference for Trinidad and Tobago by presenting conference reports every night to an eager public waiting back home. As a result, he was invited to join the BBC's Caribbean Service, part of the Overseas Service, as a producer in 1969; this acted as an important bridge between the emergent Black community in London and their countries of origin. McDonald joined ITN in 1973 and worked as a sports correspondent and a diplomatic correspondent, eventually becoming the anchor of the ITN's flagship news programme *News at Ten* in 1992. He was made an OBE in 1992 and published his autobiography, *Fortunate Circumstances*, the following year. He has written biographies of the cricketers Vivian Richards and Clive Lloyd.

Dame Jocelyn Barrow OBE. Jocelyn Barrow's career reflects her deep commitment to community relations and social justice. She was a founder member and later General Secretary of the Campaign Against Racial Discrimination, which was responsible for campaigning for the introduction of the 1968 Race Relations Act, and a member of the Community Relations Council from 1968 to 1972. In 1972 she was awarded the OBE for her work in the fields of education and community relations. Her international role as the most senior Black member of the European Commission, sitting on the Economic and Social Committee among others, was foreshadowed by her position as Vice-President of the International Human Rights Year in 1968. She was the first Black Governor of the BBC (1981–8) and Deputy Chairman of the Broadcasting Standards Council (1989–95). She became a Dame of the British Empire in 1992.

Oliver Tambo, President of the African National Congress in the 1980s. During his exile from South Africa he settled in London. In 1979 he was the first leader of a liberation movement to be honoured by a Special Committee of the United Nations; this marked the beginning of the formal recognition of African liberation movements by the UN.

̄ambo (left) shakes hands with Ken Livingstone, Leader of the Greater London Council, at an Anti-Apartheid rally in ̄rafalgar Square, 1985. The Black American community leader Jesse Jackson is in the centre.

Rally outside the house in New Cross where thirteen young Black people died in the arson attack of January 1981. After the fire, John La Rose and others set up the New Cross Massacre Action Committee to support bereaved parents and to demand a full police investigation. The committee organized the Black People's Day of Action in 1982 to demonstrate against the lack of measures taken by the police in the early investigation of the fire. It turned out to be one of the largest ever demonstrations of Black people in Britain. After a public meeting held at Deptford Town Hall (below), a procession led by the parents of the victims marched to the house in New Cross on the anniversary of the fire.

Parents of some of the victims of the New Cross massacre at a memorial service held at St Mary's Church, Lewisham, in January 1987.

Councillor Jean Bernard, Brixton, 1989, eight years after the first riots which devastated the borough. The Brixton riots were the culmination of a police/community relations crisis that went back many years; above all, they were a reaction to insensitive methods of policing which alienated an entire class of Black young people in attempting to deal with a criminal minority in this multicultural community. The injustices created by blanket police operations, which treated the innocent as if they were guilty, generated solidarity among young people, and later the whole community, who were already sharing the experiences of racism and social exclusion from the school to the world of work. The report of Lord Scarman, who led the public inquiry into the causes of the riots, validated much of what young people had been saying for years about their unfair treatment at the hands of the police. The report also documented the social, economic and environmental problems of the area, which have gradually improved with inward investment by companies.

Demonstration against the death of Colin Roach in police custody, January 1983. Colin Roach's suspicious death at Stoke Newington police station was another example of the abuse of the so-called 'Sus' laws, under which an individual could be charged with suspicious conduct. They were intended as a deterrent to crime but in practice, because of their vagueness and the biased way they were enforced, became a civil liberties nightmare for Black youth. The death of Roach was only one in a long line of Black deaths in police custody. Other victims included Trevor Morville and Tunde Hassan, who also died at Stoke Newington police station.

The mother of Cherry Groce protests outside Stoke Newington police station about Groce's shooting by police in her own home in 1985. The shooting triggered the Brixton riots. John La Rose, publisher, quotes the frequently heard statement of youth outrage: 'They are killing our mothers now.'

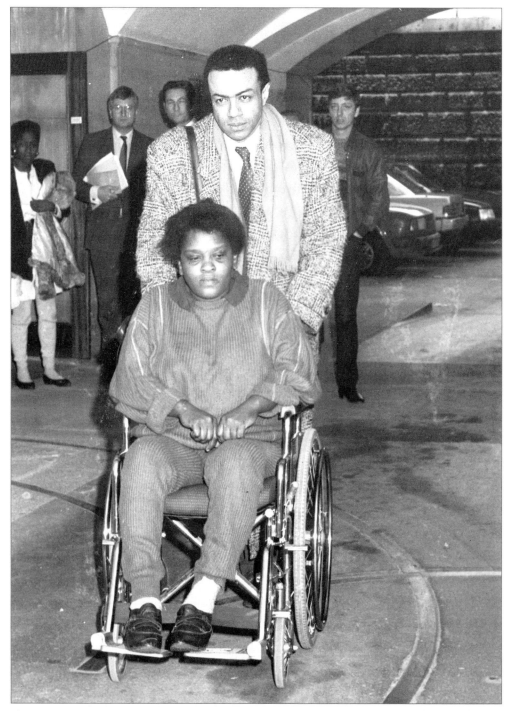

Cherry Groce being pushed by her solicitor, Paul Boateng, outside the Old Bailey during the Broadwater Farm youth trials, 1986. Cherry Groce was shot by police as they burst into her house in Brixton in 1985, looking for her son. This act, combined with the continued harassment of (mainly Black) youth by the police, triggered the second Brixton riots of September 1985 (*see* photograph opposite, top), four years after violence had previously rocked the borough.

A burnt out furniture store in Greasham Road, Brixton, 1985.

A demonstration of the Broadwater Farm Defence Campaign, 1985 (opposite). A week after the Brixton riots of 1985, a middle-aged Black woman, Mrs Cynthia Jarrett, died from heart failure after being pushed by a policeman searching her house in an illegal police raid. The police had entered her house without a warrant, using keys taken from her son while he was in police custody; he had been arrested for a simple motoring offence and no longer lived at home. This incident, one of many cited by the Institute of Race Relations throughout the 1980s as evidence of the abuse of police powers to enter homes in the Black community, triggered the Tottenham riots of 1985 in which PC Blakelock was killed. After the riots the Broadwater Farm Defence Campaign was set up to defend local youth against police reprisal. In 1988 this campaign was co-ordinated by Janet Clarke (above).

The Africa Centre at the heart of Covent Garden, opened by Kenneth Kaunda, President of Zambia, in 1964, has provided a window into Africa for both Black and White Londoners for nearly forty years. It has hosted speakers from all over Africa, including exiles, leaders and future leaders of African states, and acted as the prime location for the organization of political events and as the meeting point for rallies and demonstrations. In 1994 the Organization of African Unity proposed to support the centre in its mission to create a 'flagship for Africa in Europe' and to develop its conference and leisure facilities in a new architectural scheme. This picture taken on 13 April 1970 shows, left to right, Mrs George, Miss Waller, Mrs Wilson, Mrs Adu, Mrs Oguumowo, Chief Mrs Jones, Chief Mrs Manuwa and Miss ?.

A language class at the Africa Centre in the early 1960s. Since its inception, the Africa Centre has enriched the intellectual life of the capital, with academics and intellectuals discussing their work, teaching and giving master classes. African women have played a significant part in the workings of the centre. In 1986, the late Sally Mugabe, political activist and wife of the president of Zimbabwe, hosted Focus on African Women. The centre's book fairs and art exhibitions have made a major contribution to awareness of African culture in the UK.

Rt Revd Desmond Tutu addressing the Nelson Mandela Freedom March to London, Hyde Park, 1988. This rally was typical of the Anti-Apartheid movement at the height of its activity in the 1980s as it focused on the demand for Mandela to be released. The movement itself was born in 1959 as a response to the brutal racist regime in South Africa. It protested against the Sharpeville Massacre of 1960 and all the atrocities and outrages that followed with a mixture of demonstrations, lobbying and economic and cultural boycotts. The photo below shows demonstrators at an Anti-Apartheid rally in London in 1982.

Scenes from the Notting Hill Carnival. The Notting Hill Carnival was founded by Claudia Jones in 1959 after the Notting Hill riots to foster better relations between the Black and White communities. Throughout the 1950s and '60s, the Black community was under physical attack from racist gangs and faced hostility from a White community whose insecurities were being fed by misinformation about the new 'alien culture' in its midst. Today Carnival celebrates Britain's cultural diversity.

Carnival is a festival originating in the West Indies, where slaves used masquerade, costume, dance and spectacle as the only opportunity for political comment, encoded through humour and caricature. Today carnival in the West Indies marks Lent, the gathering of crops, independence from colonial rule and the emancipation from slavery. Slaves who participated in carnival in the West Indies drew their inspiration from much earlier African traditions which deployed masquerade and spectacle for political commentary in festivals such as 'Gelede' from the Yorubas of Nigeria.

Although the Notting Hill Carnival began on a small scale (the 1961 Carnival took place in the Lyceum ballroom on the Strand), it is now the biggest and most famous street festival in Europe, attracting crowds in excess of a million and celebrating the ethnic diversity of British society. It is co-ordinated by a Carnival and Arts Committee, whose officers span the worlds of the arts, business, community work, broadcasting and politics. Public funding from local authorities and arts institutions signifies the recognition of the role that the Carnival plays in the economic and cultural life of London.

Claire Holder, who has been responsible for organizing the Notting Hill Carnival since 1989. In recent years, the need to realize the Carnival's commercial potential has often clashed with the demand to preserve its dynamic and subversive essence and its spiritual value. So while some recognize how much the Carnival contributes to tourism and the opportunities afforded to Black businesses, the Association for a People's Carnival decries the commercialization and cultural dilution of Carnival, its hijacking by big institutions and its appropriation by arts administrators, museums and academics. By bowing to market forces, has Carnival benefited big business more than the community? The argument – like Carnival – still rages.

ACKNOWLEDGEMENTS

I give my special thanks to all those who have made this book possible and whose participation suggests that they too have seen the need to tell these human stories in a way with which people can more clearly identify:

West Africa magazine, the keeper of the torch in relation to the history of Black London since 1917, both African and West Indian. I extend my special thanks to its editor, Maxwell Nwagboso, deputy editor, Desmond Davis, general manager, Kaye Whiteman, and illustrator and photographic archivist, Tayo Fatunla, whose historical appreciation led their support in the research of this book and whose own knowledge was a spur to enquiries even further afield.

Mr Arif Ali, original proprietor of the *Caribbean Times* since 1981 and the *West Indian Digest* since 1971, who had the foresight to maintain an archive and whose Hansib publications are a must for all researchers of the Black experience in modern Britain. Special thanks to Mr Ross Slater, news editor of the *Caribbean Times* and *New Nation*, for his early and continued support, and Mr Tetteh Kofi, managing editor of the *New Nation* for the Ethnic Media Group's continued commitment to the project.

The West Indian Ex-Servicemen's (and Women's) Association and its members have been an invaluable historical resource in areas which extend far beyond the military. Posthumously, I would like to thank Mr Kelly, a debonair ex-serviceman and civil servant, whose testimony was particularly moving. Also I thank Mr Webb, the current president, Mr Phillpotts and Mr Flanigan, education and publicity officers, whose knowledge is encyclopaedic.

Colonel Christine Moody and Cynthia Moody, keepers of the torch of the earlier history of Black London, whose own outstanding achievements and dedication to the legacy of the Moody family has been an inspiration.

The London Transport Museum's Hugh Robertson and Felicity Premru have enabled me to include a significant chapter on employment history and the early pattern of modern immigration. I am grateful to them.

Thanks to Mr Christopher Shokoya-Eleshin of Shokoya-Eleshin Construction Ltd; Terence Pepper of the National Portrait Gallery; Mrs Watley-Barrow of the Barbados Museum and Historical Archive; Mr Gbenga Sonuga, former senior archivist and director of the Calabar Museum and Lagos Arts Council, Nigeria; Mr Julian Watson and Ms Francis Ward; Mr C.B. Mears and Mr W. Ryder for their contributions to the history of Black people in Greenwich.

Finally, I would like to thank my sisters Elizabeth and Josephine Okokon, who are probably unaware of the extent to which their support and encouragement have carried me through this project.

PICTURE CREDITS

The author would like to thank the following for permission to use their photographs – (T) = top of page, (B) = bottom of page: Africa Centre Library and Archive, pp. 108, 122; Barbados Museum and Historical Society Archive, pp. 6, 10, 34; BFI Films, pp. 18; Paul Boateng MP, p. 72; Stephen Bourne Collection, pp. 2, 16, 17; Mr Jack Bubuela-Dodd, p. 57(B); *Caribbean Times*, pp. 20(B), 21(B), 22, 25, 68, 69, 70, 74, 86, 90(T), 110, 112(T), 115, 118 – Anna Arone, p. 90(B) – Rod Leon, pp. 42, 55, 56 – Humphrey Newmar, pp. 116, 117, 120 – Anni Silvgrleaf pp. 3, 123 – Julian Smith, p. 113 – Andrew Wiard, *Report*, p. 70; Coalition Records, courtesy of *Caribbean Times*, p. 27(T); C. Cole, p. 35 (T right); Derron Curtis, p. 39(B); Mr Ben Davis, p. 95(T); Mrs Joyce Edwards, p. 96(B); Mrs Hilda Egonu, Uzo Egonu Archive, p. 13; Mr Neil Flanigan (WIESA), p. 40(B); Mrs Constance Goodridge-Mark, p. 35(T left); Greenwich Local History Archive, pp. 33, 44, 45, 102; Professor Ian Hall, p. 26(T); Hansib Publications, pp. 7, 114 – Humphrey Newmar, p. 73, 91, 121, 125, 126(B); Mrs Isobel Husbands, p. 57(T); Charles Ifejika, p. 106(B); ITN, p. 111; Mr Buzz Johnson, Claudia Jones Archive, p. 67; Mrs K.A.M. King-Okokon, p. 49, 84(B); Larkin Bros, London, pp. 1, 24; Gloria Lock, p. 106(T); London Transport Museum, pp. 94, 95(T), 96, 97, 98(B), 99(B), 100; Mrs Audrey McCracken, p. 46; *Mirror*, p. 82; Colonel Charles Arundel Moody, p. 36(T); Dr Christine Moody, pp. 29, 47, 48, 92(T) ; Cynthia Moody, pp. 21(T); Black filmmaker publications, p. 20(T); Museum of London, p. 53, 88; National Portrait Gallery, p. 60, 89; New Beacon Publications, p. 107(B); Nichols Employment Agency, p. 56; Ms Elizabeth Okokon, p. 50(B); Mr Laurie Phillpotts (WIESA), p. 41; Andrew Putler, p. 26(B); Royal College of Music, p. 23; Mrs Shirlene Rudder MBE, p. 50(T); Savana Picture Library, p. 107(T); Delma Scott-Dixon, p. 38; Mr Christopher Shokoya-Eleshin, pp. 58–9; Sport & General Press Agency Ltd, courtesy of *West Africa Journal*, p. 76; TUC, p. 61(T); UNISON, p. 61(B); Mr Rudolph Walker, p. 19; London Borough of Wandsworth Libraries, p. 65; Mr Hector Watson (WIESA), p. 40(T); *West Africa* Magazine Archive, pp. 12, 15, 28, 54, 77, 78, 79, 80, 81, 83, 84(T), 85, 104(B), 105, 112(B), 123(T), 124; West Indian Ex-Servicemen's (and Women's) Association (WIESA), p. 35(B), 36(B), 37; Mr A.O. Williamson-Taylor, p. 62; Mr Lionel Yard, Amy Ashwood Garvey Archive, p. 66.

While every effort has been made to credit the copyright holders for all the pictures in this book, this has not always been possible. The author would like to apologize for any omission.

INDEX